RAMBLES ARO

Cover: View from footpath just below Coombe Hatch (see Walk 11)

Rambles around
NEWTON ABBOT

*featuring Abbotskerswell, Bishopsteignton,
Bovey Tracey, Chudleigh, Coffinswell,
Combeinteignhead, Denbury, Highweek,
Ideford, Ipplepen, Kingsteignton, Milber,
the Ogwells and Teignmouth*

Roger Jones

Illustrations by Leonard Dawkins

EX LIBRIS PRESS

First published in 1980 by Roger Jones
This edition, revised and reset, published in 1992 by
EX LIBRIS PRESS
1 The Shambles
Bradford on Avon
Wiltshire

Typeset in 10 point Palatino

Design and typesetting by Ex Libris Press

Cover printed by Shires Press, Trowbridge
Printed and bound in Great Britain by
Dotesios Ltd., Trowbridge, Wiltshire

ISBN 0 948578 40 8

CONTENTS

Everything in the world can be better seen by the walker on foot than by any other person; there is an intimate communion with the life of the country, a leisurely unrolling of the scene, a sense of being let into the secrets of the life which flows around one, deep and steady and enduring .... No one, I think, knows the true joy of the country who does not know the joy of walking; even its difficulties have their reward: the struggle against a bleak head-wind on an uphill road, and the sense of peace when one drops into a sheltered valley where the early primroses are yellow in the hedges .... How good is the taste of food after long hours of walking! How good to stretch one's limbs, in winter to the blaze of a fire, in summer in the cool shade of a garden! How calm and contented is the mind, and full of quiet and pleasant thoughts!

John Presland
Torquay: the charm and history of its neighbourhood, 1920

Introduction

It was in March 1992 that a local bookseller prompted the notion that I should produce a new edition of *Rambles Around Newton Abbot*, a book which I had originally published in 1980, less than a year after the appearance of my *A Book of Newton Abbot* and a few months before I left the town for Wiltshire. I dug out a copy of the original book and, upon reading it, soon became immersed in half remembered details of the footpaths and countryside around Newton Abbot.

With the approach of spring each year, the old restlessness creeps upon me – the longing to step out for a spot of serious walking, to fill the lungs with fresh air and to partake of the boundless new life of the growing season. What better than to retrace the walks I had originally charted and trodden in 1978-79? Thus it was, that for six days in the merry month of May, I paid two visits to South Devon to do just that, and more. The first long weekend – May Day Bank Holiday – was blessed with bright sunshine and a cool breeze: perfect walking weather, and I reckon I walked around sixty miles in four days. I came home footsore but inspired and invigorated. I returned a couple of weeks later on a weekend when spring changed suddenly to high summer (it was hot!) in order to walk the two longest routes: from Newton Abbot to Bovey Tracey and Teignmouth respectively.

The great difference in one's impression of the villages and countryside around Newton Abbot in 1992 as compared to 1979 is the fact that there has been such an enormous amount of new building in that time. Kingsteignton, Milber, Kingskerswell, Abbotskerswell, Ipplepen, East Ogwell and Chudleigh, as well as Newton Abbot itself, have all grown hugely. The population must have soared – new schools and roads have been opened up. No doubt South Devon is a desirable place to live, but one is left puzzling over the question of where all these newcomers work.

Because of the peculiar topography of this part of South Devon, namely, its closely jumbled hills and vales, it is still easy to distinguish one community from another. But one feels that there cannot be much room left for further expansion around those aforementioned centres. If it does happen, then Torbay and Newton Abbot will merge into some Greater South Devon. On the other hand, some villages have escaped mainly free of new development. Denbury and Torbryan remain unspoilt gems, as very largely do Coffinswell and Combe-inteignhead. I stayed in Luton which, with its sister village of Ideford, lies below Little Haldon and enjoys a rural seclusion not only beyond the reach of the developers but also the noise pollution of the A38 and A380 which affects so many villages betwixt Dartmoor and the coast.

I set out to retrace all the routes in my original book and to establish a couple of shorter walks close to Newton Abbot. What I had not realised was how long some of my routes had been. I have subsequently shortened several or offered shorter alternatives. (That I found my routes long may have something to do with my being somewhat older). In addition, it is always possible to shorten routes by arranging to be picked up at some convenient point. I have tried very hard to avoid walking along main roads or along any roads where there is a significant amount of traffic. With a greater population has come an increased volume of traffic and increased hazards for the pedestrian.

There is not, it must be said, a comprehensive network of footpaths within the six or seven mile radius of Newton Abbot which this book seeks to explore. This is probably because there are so many good old Devon lanes: the high-banked, single-carriageway thoroughfares which serve none but local farms and habitations. Many miles walking along such ways are included here and for that I make no apology. The traffic is likely to be extremely light. Because of the prevailing quietude, when a vehicle does approach, one hears its approach long before it passes or one spots it bobbing over the hill-top ahead. At the time I walked these routes, in May, the lane walking was an absorbing pleasure on account of the extraordinary wild flower richness of the hedgebanks – an endless floral display.

Much to my delight I found excellent access to rights of way, with very few exceptions. Devon County Council seem to have systematically signposted all the local footpaths and erected stout wooden stiles to aid the rambler at crossing points. Not only this, but new footpaths have been created where before there were none, for example, the useful stretch which links Penn Inn with the River Teign (see Walk 7). Teignbridge District Council, too, obviously shows great concern for the various parcels of countryside for which it has responsibility. Take Decoy Lake just south of Newton Abbot. I remember it as an abandoned and overgrown former industrial site. Now it is a well landscaped area managed to provide a natural environment and to offer leisure activities, such as sailing and windsurfing, for other users as well as walkers. Or take Orley Common between Ipplepen and Torbryan – an extensive area of common land, well wooded but made accessible, even welcoming, by the provision of a discreet car park on one side of the lane and information boards on the other. It is far from being regimented and overorganised – one simply senses a gentle helping hand. Even Newton Abbot Town Council have erected notices on their patch of the recently created Templer Way warning would be offenders that the depositing of litter is an offence and that perpetrators of this foul deed will not only be fined but their names published. In the present mood, it would not surprise me if the Town Council re-established the stocks beside St. Leonard's Tower for the ritual chucking of rotten tomatoes at such anti-social evil-doers!

To sum up, the authorities seem to show real concern for the environment and genuinely to be serving the community in this respect. With its exemplary system for recycling rubbish, Devon would appear to be a very green county. I note that even the Teignbridge District Council leaflet on 'Guided Walks and Activities in Teignbridge' is printed on recycled paper. More strength to all their elbows!

One of the very few flies in the ointment is Old Milber Lane, the enclosed footpath which begins at the top of Milber Woods and eventually drops down to Coffinswell. No sooner does one begin to enjoy the route than it is barred off by a sign proclaiming, DANGER – QUARRY. This is not before passing a sign which invites the rambler across a field, courtesy of the farmer, in order to avoid this major obstacle. The sand and gravel quarry, Aller Vale, has extended its workings back into the hillside, swallowing up a chunk of old Milber Lane in the process.

As I wrote in the Introduction to the first edition of this book, it was coming to live in Newton Abbot in 1976 that first opened my eyes to the pleasures and possibilities of walking in the countryside. As a Londoner born and bred, it was simply something I had never done before. Ordnance Survey maps were another discovery and I set out to walk all the off-road rights of way around the town that I could identify. To return to those introductory paragraphs written in December 1979:

There is an incredible variety of terrain within a small radius of the town, this variety created by the complex geology of the region. This in turn gives rise to a wide range of agricultural and industrial uses and to enormous variety in such things as the occurrence of wild flowers. I feel I have discovered this district for myself and in so doing I have found immense pleasure. I hope that, in setting down these rambles on paper, I will not detract from that sense of discovery in others.

In preparing this book, I have tried to provide more than just a guide along some suggested routes. I hope that the historical and other passages will give added interest and prompt the rambler to delve further. The 'Gleanings' are a selection of vignettes which reveal places as seen by travellers of earlier times. Leonard Dawkins' attractive sketches offer a valuable record for all who enjoy these rambles.

The resultant book is therefore something of a pot pourri but, I hope, one which will prove useful and informative and of enjoyment to the armchair rambler as well as to those on foot.

May you enjoy these walks as much as I did in completing them in preparation of this new edition.

Roger Jones
June 1992

A Note on the Maps and Directions

The maps which accompany the rambles in this book are by no means definitive but merely sketch maps which plot the course of the rambles and distinguish between road, track and footpath. Nevertheless, together with the detailed directions offered in the text, they should be sufficient to guide the rambler along the various routes described.

My starting point for charting these walks was the Ordnance Survey 1:25,000 Pathfinder maps. All the routes in this book are included on two maps, as follows:

Pathfinder 1342 : Newton Abbot
Pathfinder 1351 : Torbay

These are superb maps for the purpose of cross country walking; they are sufficiently detailed to delineate the field boundaries as well as every structure right down to the humblest field barn. On the other hand, the current editions are somewhat dated. New paths have been created, old ones rerouted – I have pointed out where this has happened. One may not be able to take the current edition of the Pathfinder maps as gospel but they are immensely interesting and useful and should be acquired by any serious walker.

Key to the sketch maps:

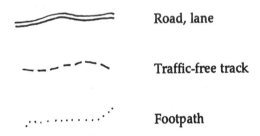

Road, lane

Traffic-free track

Footpath

|| In the text I have distinguished the passages which describe the route, as opposed to commentary on things seen, by indenting and highlighting with a double vertical line, like this paragraph.

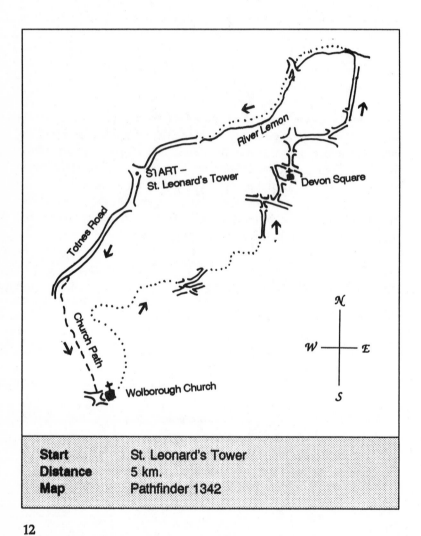

Start	St. Leonard's Tower
Distance	5 km.
Map	Pathfinder 1342

1
NEWTON ABBOT CIRCULAR
via Wolborough, Courtenay Park and River Lemon

Going: This is a semi-urban walk but one which provides an essential introduction to the town south of the River Lemon, the landmark which once divided the twin settlements of Newton Bushel (Highweek – to the north) and Newton Abbot (Wolborough – to the south). The field path along the steep north slope of Wolborough Hill could be regarded as Newton Abbot's most classic walk. Cows graze on the green hillside which seems to thrust its way into the town. The views are extensive and help us understand the shape and extent of the town.

From St. Leonard's you begin the walk by heading south-west-wards along Wolborough Road. Immediately past the impressive facade of Mackrell's Almshouses you leave the road by bearing left along the traffic-free Church Path. Follow this way until you eventually emerge at Wolborough Church which is generally kept locked. A notice informs that the key is obtainable at the nearby farm and is well worth a small detour.

From Wolborough Church take the track which follows the churchyard wall towards a kissing gate. Go through here and follow the beaten path – not the track which ascends the slope straight ahead – the path which curves off to the left on an even contour. Follow this around the promontory, then descend a little towards the bench seat and follow the path around the hill until you emerge onto Powderham Road.

Bear left here, ignoring the steps on your left. Just past the large modern house named Ionia, look out for a Public Footpath sign on the right. Follow this narrow boundary path until you reach a T-junction. Now turn left to descend the hill to meet Western Road. Turn right and left down Hilton Road. Turn right and cross the road (East Street) and left into Devon Square. You can cut through the square on which the Victorian St. Paul's Church stands and continue past Newton Abbot Town Council offices and the Town Museum.

For the sake of seeing more of the town, bear right here, towards the station, then left along Quay Road (in the direction of the former Newton Abbot Quay), then bear left along Teign Road and the impressive bulk of Tuckers Maltings (since 1991 open to the public and well worth seeing). The rectangle of green on the left is Osborne Park; the recently built flats further on were erected on the site of the former Newton Abbot Power Station.

Bear left at the River Lemon, cross the old footbridge and bear left beside the river, then right and left along Wharf Road. Cross over The Avenue, and follow Marsh Road beside the Lemon. This will take you as far as Hero Bridge where the river is culverted beneath the town. From here you can head down Courtenay Street to reach St. Leonard's Tower.

Looking back to Wolborough church from the footpath

Kissing gate beside Wolborough churchyard wall.
Go through here and bear left, not straight on.

Wolborough Church is dedicated to St. Mary. Its fabric is mainly fifteenth century perpendicular, though the font and tower are earlier. The interior is both beautiful and interesting but you will normally have to obtain the key to enter from Wolborough Farm. St. Leonard's Tower, the starting point of this walk, is a remnant of St. Leonard's Church, once a chapel-of-ease to St. Mary's.

Mackrell's Almshouses were endowed by one Thomas Mackrell, a son of Newton Abbot who, as a child, played at this spot. He made his fortune as a chemist in Barnstaple. The original terrace was erected in 1874, the other in exactly the same style by his sister in 1894, as can be surmised by a close inspection of the commemorative plaques set in the stonework.

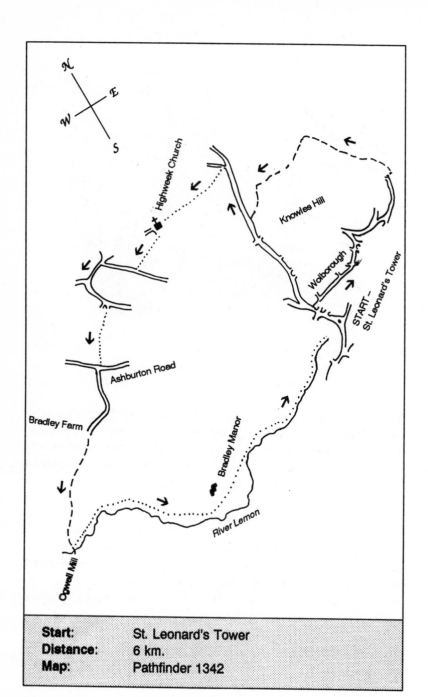

N

E

W

S

Highweek Church

Knowles Hill

Wolborough

START –
St. Leonard's Tower

Ashburton Road

Bradley Farm

Bradley Manor

River Lemon

Ogwell Mill

Start:	St. Leonard's Tower
Distance:	6 km.
Map:	Pathfinder 1342

2
NEWTON ABBOT CIRCULAR
via Knowles Hill, Highweek and Ogwell Mill

Going: Another semi-town walk, this route explores parts of Newton Abbot which lie on the north side of the River Lemon. Knowles Hill mirrors Wolborough Hill, with its Victorian villas. Highweek, identified by its parish church on the highest point, forms a westerly extension of Knowles Hill, though the two are bisected by the Bovey Tracey Road. The route abruptly leaves built-up Newton Abbot and follows the charming green lane past Barton Farm to reach the former Ogwell Mill; from this point we turn back to town by following the riverside path.

From St. Leonard's Tower head up Bank Street, past the magnificently restored facade of the School of Art and Public Library, and along Highweek Street. Bear right up Chapel Hill. Now you are in the midst of Abbotsbury, built in the Edwardian period in the former grounds of Abbotsbury House. Head straight along Fisher Road, cross Abbotsbury Road and follow Bury Road opposite.

Cross Knowles Hill Road and proceed along Rundle Road until it peters out into a footpath. Do not take the footpath, however, but descend the 82 steps towards the roundabout on the Kingsteignton Road. Turn left, past the B & Q warehouse and follow Jetty Marsh Lane past various works and an old quarry in the north side of Knowles Hill. Eventually the track takes a left hand bend and follows a high stone wall – the boundary of Sandford Orleigh – to emerge on the main road from Newton Abbot to Bovey Tracey. This road is always busy so DO TAKE CARE in crossing it to reach the pavement on the far side.

Turn right and follow the pavement for a short distance until you reach the track leading off on your left. Leave the main road here by turning left up the footpath – not the drive by the gatehouse to the right. This is a fragment of the old coffin path which once linked Highweek Church to Kingsteignton Parish Church. This pleasant path beats a steady ascent towards Highweek Church, which occupies a wonderfully peaceful hill-top site, a perfect place to pause and take in the views by walking around the churchyard which surrounds the church itself.

Leave by the lych gate on the far side and bear left by the indicated Public Footpath, then right by the remains of a kissing gate.

View down the Teign estuary from footpath beside Highweek Church

Turn right at the road and climb up to Highweek Inn. Bear left and left again into Coombeshead Road. Just past Castlewood Avenue look out for a Public Footpath sign on your right. Follow this old way between private gardens to the Ashburton Road. Cross over (take care!) and walk straight ahead until you reach Bradley Farm on the right. At this point the tarmac ends and the lane gradually descends to the well wooded valley of the River Lemon.

You reach the river at the former Ogwell Mill, now a private house. Turn left here and follow the path beside the Lemon, then the mill leat, first across a meadow, then through the woods and the meadow beside the boundary wall of Bradley Manor.

There are various ways of reaching St. Leonard's Tower but, for the sake of staying away from roads, it is worth following the leat side and riverside paths. To do so: follow the leat from Bradley Manor until it eventually disappears underground, then take the path which follows the left bank of the Lemon, all the way to Union Bridge from which point St. Leonard's Tower is visible to the right.

Highweek Church, as seen emerging from the old coffin path

Highweek Church, dedicated to All Saints, was built in the early fifteenth century by Richard Yarde of Bradley Manor. Before the building of the new church, there existed a chapel-of-ease to Kingsteignton Church, so that Highweek was included in the Parish of Kingsteignton and remained so until 1864. The chapel had no burial ground and the local dead were transported, via the path followed in this walk, to Kingsteignton.

Ogwell Mill, demolished after World War 2, was a watermill fed by a leat from the Lemon. The old mill was a famous beauty spot and appears in countless old photographs and paintings.

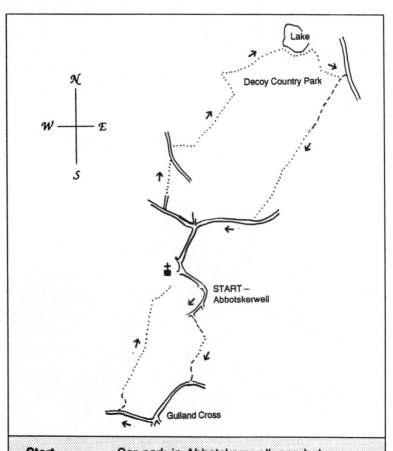

Start	Car park in Abbotskerswell, see below.
Distance	7 km, or 5 km omitting southerly loop.
Getting there	From Newton Abbot take the Totnes Road and turn left for Abbotskerswell.
Parking	Abbotskerswell has a small public car park. Follow the main street through the village and keep going – look out for a playground on your left; there is a parking area just beside the road at this point.
Bus	75A
Map	Pathfinders 1342, 1351
Reference	858686

3
ABBOTSKERSWELL CIRCULAR
via Decoy Country Park

Going: This is a comparatively short and undemanding walk from the village of Abbotskerswell, through fields and Decoy Country Park, then by track, field path and lane back to the starting point. It is a simple straightforward route which offers some tremendous views and great variety.

The first section of the walk, which describes a southerly loop to include tracks, lanes and field paths, could be regarded as an optional extra. It adds a couple of kilometres but is a pleasant diversion and is a way of discovering more of Abbotskerswell and its environs.

Optional southerly loop:
With your back to the car park turn left. Bear right at the Butchers Arms pub and proceed along the unmade track signposted as a Public Bridleway. Follow this past Ladywell – notice the well itself before reaching the house.

The Ladywell, or Ladewell, is a kind of stone box built around a bowl which is fed by a spring issuing at this very spot; the stream running beside the path is the overflow from the bowl.

Continue along the right of way, first an enclosed track, then a wider, more open way until you reach the lane where you bear right to Gulland Cross. Bear right again and look out for a signposted Bridleway on your right. Follow this hedged track until you find a stile on your right. Cross into the field and head towards a pair of stiles in the far hedgebank. Climb over these and

Ladywell, Abbotskerswell

keep heading in the same direction – this will lead you towards a stone wall, enclosing a wood, which you follow on your right. Leave the field beside the entrance gate to the RNID College (Royal National Institute for the Deaf). Head for the grassy path which can be found just to the left of the gatepost and drop down to the village. Cross Grange Road. Notice the Court Farm Inn on your left, the church and the Church House, all of which are worth exploring.

The Parish Church of St. Mary's is an ancient edifice though relatively small, consisting of nave and one aisle; inside there is a fifteenth century screen and medieval statue of Our Lady.

Next door to the church stands the Court Farm Inn, originally one of Abbotskerswell's farms and now a pub. Inscribed on a stone set in the wall of the room above the porch are the words, 'This house was rebuilt by James Tucket the Elder, Anno Domini 1724'. James Tucket was an Elder in the Society of Friends (Quakers) and Court Farm was for many years a refuge for members of that religion. Meeting for Worship was held in that small room above the porch.

Behind Court Farm Inn, in the left hand corner of a bend in Wilton Way, can be found the old walls of a Quaker burial ground with a commemorative plaque explaining its origin and spared the recent housing development which has engulfed the village.

The Church House is a feature common to many villages visited in this book – we encounter others at Combeinteignhead and Torbryan, where they are now a private residence and pub respectively. The Abbotskerswell Church House is host to all sorts of village groups and activities, as can be surmised from the notice-boards outside.

<u>Main Route of the Walk:</u>

If you are beginning from the car park – turn right, back towards the village centre. Or, from the Church House, head along the main street northwards. In either case head past the village stores and school and bear left up Ford Road. Carry on up Laburnham Terrace to the stile at the end. Once in the field continue to head in the same direction, just to the right of the two large oak trees, up and across the field to reach a stile in the far corner. Turn left along the lane but very soon cross a stile on the right. Follow the hedge on your right. As soon as you pass the corner of the hedgerow the view eastward suddenly opens up: there is Milber, Aller Vale Quarry and Kingskerswell.

Look out for a signpost near the hill-top on your left and climb up to this. As you do so the view opens out, equally suddenly, towards the north and west: there is Wolborough Church and Highweek Church and, on the southern flank of Wolborough Hill, a range of (mainly) Victorian villas amid the arboreal delights of this rather exclusive part of Newton Abbot. This is a good spot to orientate yourself with many of the hills and communities around Newton.

23

To continue the walk: drop down the sharp slope, in the direction of Wolborough, to the stile below and progress along the edge of the field with the wood on your right. Climb the stile in the corner and turn left along the track through the wood. At the edge of the wood you will see another Public Footpath sign – take the way to the right, cross the stile and follow the beaten path through the field with the wood on your right and Wolborough Hill to your left. Enter the wood once more and carry on in the same general direction until you reach the southern rim of Decoy Lake.

Decoy Lake is a flooded pit where ball clay was once dug. In recent years the lake and surroundings have been sensitively landscaped to provide a centre for walking and water sports. A leaflet on Decoy Country Park, as the area is now known, is available from the Tourist Information Centre in Newton Abbot, among other places, and illustrates the footpaths in the area.

The footpath emerges onto a gravel path – there is a football pitch ahead. Turn right to follow the boundary of the wood on your right and cross the rugby pitch. At a point where the terrace of houses in Decoy Road ends you will spot a Public Footpath sign pointing to the right. Go this way along an enclosed track – woods on your right and fields beyond the hedges to your left. Cross the stile ahead to enter a field and follow the hedge on your left, continuing to rise gently. Cross another stile and look out for a plank bridge across the field-side ditch – climb the stile and head to the right of an old barn. Climb the stone steps and stile, head to the right and follow the hedgebank on your right. About two-thirds of the way to the far boundary tractor tracks veer leftward, so does the right of way. This brings you to a stile in the far corner. Join the lane (to the left of the drive) and bear right towards Abbotskerswell.

There are wide views across the village from this elevated lane; at a glance the village can appear to be a great expanse of modern housing with green hills rising on every side. But the grey bulk of the old church, right at the heart of the village, will reassure that Abbotskerswell predates the building boom of the 1960s, 70s and 80s.

Abbotskerswell was once famous as the home of Henley's cider works (now the Watermota factory beside the Totnes Road) and many of the new houses, indeed, were built on orchards where cider apples once grew.

Kerswell means the well around which cress grows and the two Kerswells were distinguished by their owners at the time of the Domesday Survey. Kingskerswell at that time belonged to the Crown and Abbotskerswell to the Abbots of Horton (no connection with Newton Abbot).

‖ Simply follow the lane as it descends to the village stores — turn
‖ left for the car park.

Gleanings below; the Church House, Abbotskerswell above

The Church House, Abbotskerswell: Near the church is an ancient and interesting house provided for the accommodation of the parishioners from a distance who here spent their time between services: a large upper room for the women, and one below for the men.
John Murray: *A Handbook for Travellers in Devonshire,* 1887

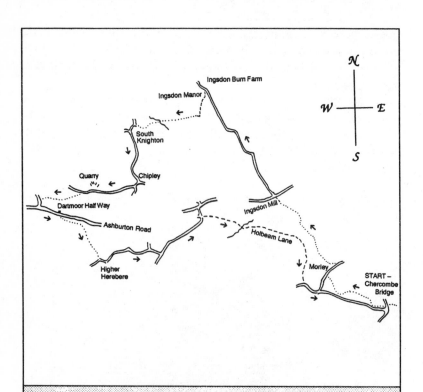

Start	Chercombe Bridge
Distance	9 km.
Getting there:	From Newton Abbot take the Ashburton Road out of town. Just past the Bradley Valley estate turn left up Chercombe Bridge Road and then down to the bridge over the Lemon.
Bus	There is no bus here but you could of course reach Chercombe Bridge by walking through Bradley Woods from Newton Abbot (see Walk 5).
Parking	There is no car park as such at Chercombe Bridge but there are a few places on the far side of the bridge where you can safely pull in off the lane.
Map	Pathfinder 1342
Reference	833711

4
CHERCOMBE BRIDGE CIRCULAR
via South Knighton, Dartmoor Half Way and Holbeam Lane

Going: This is a relatively short walk which explores a section of the River Lemon some distance upstream from Newton Abbot and the hills surrounding. There is a steady climb uphill towards Ingsdon Manor. The Dartmoor Half Way Inn lies half way along the course of this ramble, the second stage of which begins with a steep climb up a hillside to reach Higher Herebere. The route includes a variety of fieldpaths, woodland tracks, lanes and riverside paths.

On the north side of Chercombe Bridge, opposite the house, look out for a Public Footpath sign beside a stile indicating a right of way to the left. Cross into the field here and follow the path beside the River Lemon to reach the lane at Morley. Turn right and follow the lane for a short distance – as you reach the first house on the right, look out for an iron gate on your left. Enter here and follow the right of way along the edge of the wood. Eventually you leave the wood by the earth dam built across the Lemon.

The dam was built in the early 1980s as part of a scheme to control the waters of the Lemon when in spate. This followed the disastrous Newton Abbot flood of 1979. In time of flood the flow through the dam is regulated and excess water allowed to build up behind it.

Descend to the river just upstream from the dam and follow the riverside path; notice the confluence of the Kester Brook opposite. Cross a stile in the corner of this field, then pass through a gate and follow the track up towards the group of buildings, including old Ingsdon Mill, ahead. Cross the Ashburton Road (with caution) and head up the lane directly opposite. Climb steadily, past the wood on your left. Ingsdon Burn Farm will come into view on your right and the buildings of Seale-Hayne College further to the east. You eventually reach the entrance gate to the former convent school, now redeveloped following a fire and known as Ingsdon Manor.

Bear sharp left here by the signposted Public Footpath which follows the boundary wall of the Manor. Look back for a view straight down the Teign estuary to the sea before the track bears right to reach a gate. Enter the field here and follow the right of way across the summit to meet up with the field boundary on your right which descends steeply towards a stile beside a stream. Cross over and follow the enclosed path until you reach the lane at South Knighton. Turn left and begin to descend through the hamlet. Turn right past Chipley Quarry to the right of the lane, now disused but once worked for roadstone.

Ingsdon Mill

The stone here is a pillow lava – a lava which erupted on the sea-bed and cooled into characteristic pillow-like masses.

Just past the quarry look out for a Public Footpath sign on the left. Cross into the field here and follow the wide, open track to reach the lane from Bickington; now turn left for the Ashburton Road. Fortunately there in a wide grassy bank which you can walk on to reach the Dartmoor Half Way. The second stage of the walk is about to begin. Cross the road to reach a Public Footpath sign directly opposite the pub. Enter the field and head leftward, ascending slightly, to reach a stile into the wood ahead. Follow the path through the wood and emerge on the far side. You will want to pause to draw breath before tackling the steep field-slope directly ahead. Take it steadily and you will quite soon reach the gate at the very top.

Before proceeding any further it is worth pausing here to take in the view. Away to the south-east is the unmistakable eminence of Denbury Down.

Bear right to reach the lane, then left to begin the descent. Once past the entrance to Wrigwell the lane reaches a T-junction – turn left and descend again to a point near the Ashburton Road, looking out for the entrance to an unmade track on your right. Follow this track (known as Holbeam Lane), at first between fields, then across the Kester Brook and through woods, where the track rises a little. When it veers to the right you hear, and may see through the trees, the River Lemon flowing beneath the earth dam below and to your left.

As the track descends to meet the lane it becomes deeply sunken and there are outcrops of slate from whose deep crevices grow ferns and pennywort.

Bear left when you reach the lane and then, where the lane forks, either walk straight on by the lane past the former Holbeam Mill, once famous for its edge tools and fish hooks used by farmers and fishermen but now a private residence, or left towards Morley where you can retrace your steps along the riverside path linking Morley with Chercombe Bridge.

Gleanings

Bradley Woods: On either side the trees rise tier above tier, a wealth of foliage abounds everywhere, sweet scents fill the air, and the trickling of the River Lemon on one side, and the leat on the other, is the only sound, save the singing of the birds, which reveals the prevailing quietude.
A.J.Rhodes: *Newton Abbot: its History and Development*, 1904

Ingsdon House is a handsome mansion, delightfully situated on beautiful ascending ground, which commands some extensive and interesting views of the country, particularly to the south-east.
Rev. D.M. Stirling: *A History of Newton-Abbot and Newton-Bushel*, 1830

Ideford Arch – see Walk 9

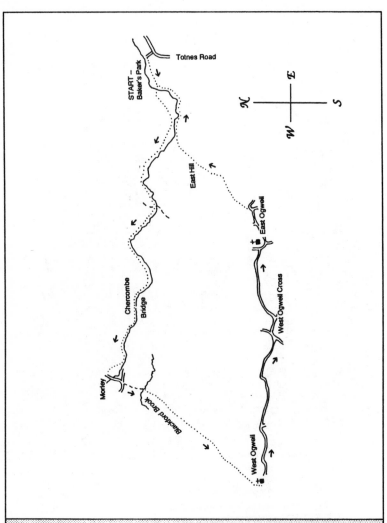

Start	Bakers Park, Totnes Road
Distance	9 km.
Parking	There is a small car park in Bakers Park which is reached via Steppes Meadow, a right turning off Totnes Road.
O.S. Map	Pathfinders 1342, 1351
Reference	853709

5
NEWTON ABBOT CIRCULAR
via Chercombe Bridge, West and East Ogwell

Going: This is an easy walk with no sharp ascents or descents and includes many footpaths through fields and woods. The going can be heavy with mud along the footpath towards West Ogwell, particularly where it crosses a brook.

Walk across Bakers Park towards Bradley Manor. Follow the path by Bradley Meadow until this path and the River Lemon converge at a gate and stile. Here you must decide whether to contiue along the main path on the right side (north bank) of the river or cross the river by the footbridge and follow the south bank. The main path is the easier route whilst the alternative path on the south bank is perhaps more of an adventure and should also be taken if you wish to visit Puritans' Pit, that great collaped cavern which once served as a place of worship for the followers of Newton Abbot's dissenting Rev. William Yeo in the seventeenth century.

The main path emerges from the woods at the weir where the mill leat originates. The low-lying field here is rather marshy and during spring abounds with marsh marigold and lady's smock.

Both paths meet at Ogwell Road (actually a track) which here crosses the River Lemon. The right hand route rises to Bradley Farm and the Ashburton Road via Bradley Barton whilst the left hand route rises to East Ogwell. The bungalow at the junction here marks the site of the former Ogwell Mill, traces of which are still visible among the old stone walls and, indeed, in the mill leat which issues into the Lemon from a large pipe where Ogwell Road fords the river.

Bridge over mill leat, Bradley Manor

You must now follow the path on the north bank across an open field backed by thick woodland on an ascending slope. Continue along this path through Broadridge Wood.

You pass by former limestone quarries and their accompanying lime kilns. If you feel so inclimed, you can climb to the top of the first one by a rough path on the right side of the quarry – the view from the summit is well worth the effort.

Carry on until you emerge onto the lane by Chercombe Bridge.

At this point you have reached the end of the Devonian limestone formation and the gorge-like course which the River Lemon, for the most part, strikes through it. Before you is more open country composed of Devonian slates locally reinforced, as in the hills behind Morley and Holbeam, with igneous rocks such as dolerite.

At Chercombe Bridge Road turn left over the Lemon. Climb up to the junction and bear left. Very shortly on the right look out for three gates – take the centre one which is indicated Public Footpath. Follow this way between hedges. Cross the stream at the bottom.

The name of this brook is given as Blackford Brook on the Pathfinder map but as Barham's Brook on the old six inch map. Here you are in limestone country, but only just. Blackford Brook runs along the line of a geological fault where the younger Devonian slates have slipped down against the older Devonian limestone on which you are standing. The hills on the far side of the valley are formed by hard, igneous rock reinforcing the soft slates against the forces of erosion.

A road runs along the opposite bank of the valley and serves the farms at Holbeam to the north; Bearah, north-west and Metley, due west. These are all visible from this point; so too are some distant peaks at the southern extremity of Dartmoor, in the vicinity of South Brent and Ivybridge.

You now climb again towards a gate. About 25 metres below, bear right through a gap between an ash and an oak tree. Now bear left and follow the hedgebank on the left.

Over the brow of the hill can be seen a stile at a point about fifty metres to the right of the far left corner. Cross the middle of the next sloping field to a gate on the opposite side; now follow the left-hand hedgerow to reach another gate beneath a row of stately horse chestnut trees. Head down slightly to a gate in the barbed wire fence. As you approach the gate you can see the tower of West Ogwell church ahead.

You have a good view of the extensive woodland, including quite a bit of coniferous, in the valley here. I guess the flat valley bottom is too waterlogged to be used for arable and that is why this territory has been given over to the cultivation of trees.

On the left, evenly spaced along the stone wall and dotted about the field are trees of a different character – trees planted for their beauty, as in a park, rather than for their economic value. The limes and sycamores and horse chestnuts suggest the close proximity of a country residence.

Very soon a large house comes into view, behind the wall on your left.

This is, or was, West Ogwell Manor House, and is now a convent. The Reynell family acquired the manor by purchase in the sixteenth century and built the present house in 1790. The view from the field is unpromising so it is a good idea to turn your attention first to the little church which nestles so prettily among the trees on the small bluff ahead.

West Ogwell Manor House

The church is small but its well proportioned tower striking and its unaltered, early English, cruciform shape interesting. This little church, so remote from any population, other than the nearby farm and convent (which has its own chapel) has been declared redundant, and is now preserved for posterity under the Redundant Churches Fund. Sir John Betjeman, in his guide to English parish churches, describes West Ogwell Church as 'delightful' and 'very appealing'.

The interior is plain, unadorned and quite unVictorianised. It is significant that writers of the Victorian and Edwardian eras should describe this church with a marked lack of enthusiasm as containing no features of interest or architectural merit but that this fact should appeal to observers of our own era.

West Ogwell Church

From the church you should turn left along the lane past the attractive eighteenth century facade of the manor house and the modern chapel on its right. Continue along the lane past the farm to West Ogwell Cross.

You can see woodland away to the right along the lane to Denbury. On the right side of the lane is Oxenham's Wood and on the left is Channings Wood which gives its name to the prison. The prison is set on a little plateau and it is interesting to learn that Short Brothers, the aircraft manufacturer, once set up a works here. No aeroplanes took off and landed, however, and it was replaced by an Army barracks, now converted to a prison.

You go straight on at West Ogwell Cross and follow the road to East Ogwell. This village is a mixture of old, well preserved cottages and recent bungalows and houses. Follow the main road down into the village; opposite the Jolly Sailor Inn stands East Ogwell Church.

This is a fourteenth century church dedicated to St. Bartholomew and is worth visiting to inspect its curious layout. The side facing the road looks as though the church has a cruciform shape, like West Ogwell. On entering the church, however, you can see that the opposite transept has been enlarged into a full aisle, the alteration being undertaken in the fifteenth century. The surviving transept contains the tomb of Richard Reynell who was Sheriff of Devon and died in 1585, and of his wife Agnes, although there is no indication of the tomb's contents.

The Reynells acquired the Manor of East Ogwell in the fourteenth century by marriage and descendants of the family later acquired West Ogwell and the Manor of Wolborough, residing at Forde House. Later still, East Ogwell passed by marriage to the Taylors and there is, near the Reynell tomb, a memorial tablet to General Reynell George Taylor who died in East Ogwell in 1886, having distinguished himself as an army officer in India.

Follow the road straight through the village until you reach the green. Head across the green to a stile composed of three steel bars fixed between limestone posts. Cross this stile and follow the path along the hedgerow on the right to another stile to reach the 92 metre summit of East Hill.

East Hill is a little limestone plateau, easy to traverse in the wettest conditions and marked by minor outcrops of grey Devonian limestone, perhaps not as impressive as the massive limestone clints of the north country but nevertheless unmistakable. The view from the top is panoramic: Dartmoor, Highweek, the Haldon Hills, Newton Abbot and Wolborough.

The exit from this hill top field can be a bit tricky to locate. If you regain your bearings and head due north towards the far edge of the field you will find a small clump of ash trees which you should pass on the left and then make for a gap in the brambles. Follow the field boundary to the far corner.

You turn left along a path which you meet at this point. This leads you through Bradley Woods, downhill all the way, until you reach the riverside path on the south bank of the Lemon. Follow the river downstream to the footbridge which carries you over the river towards Bradley Manor and Bakers Park.

Gleanings

In summer, an excursion from Newton to Churcombe-bridge ... constitutes a morning walk of incomparable interest and beauty. The route is by a clean footpath which winds along the romantic banks of the Lemmon ... *Bradley Wood* is entered; here the ear is saluted by 'music from a thousand throats'; some of the notes and intonations are, indeed, harsh, but these tend only to heighten and vary the delightful modulations and exquisite harmony, which other minstrels of the wood are pouring forth to the great and glorious author of nature.
Rev. D.M.Stirling:
A History of Newton-Abbot and Newton-Bushel, 1830

Ogwell (West) is a small parish adjoining East Ogwell, about two miles S.W. of Newton Abbot. It has only 51 souls, and some 1000 acres of land, generally fertile, and finely undulated ... A handsome seat, called Ogwell House, pleasantly situated in a small deer park, finely clothed with wood.
White's *History Gazateer and Directory of Devonshire,* 1850

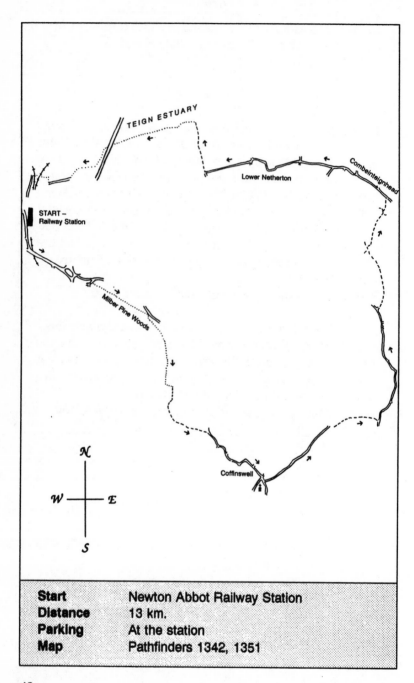

TEIGN ESTUARY

Combeinteignhead

Lower Netherton

START –
Railway Station

Milber Pine Woods

Coffinswell

N

W ——— *E*

S

Start	Newton Abbot Railway Station
Distance	13 km.
Parking	At the station
Map	Pathfinders 1342, 1351

6
NEWTON ABBOT CIRCULAR
via Coffinswell, Combeinteignhead and Lower Netherton

Going: Fairly easy, by an interesting assortment of footpaths, bridleways, tracks and lanes. The lane out of Coffinswell is moderately strenuous, rising 75 metres in about one kilometre. A high point around 165 metres is reached soon after. There is a steep descent into Combeinteignhead by a deep, sunken path which I imagine would be muddy in wet weather. If you intend to use the estuary footpath on the way back to Newton Abbot, as I have suggested, you should ensure that there is not a high tide at the time.

With your back to Newton Abbot Railway Station bear left and follow the main road to Pennin roundabout. Descend into the subway, walk straight across to emerge at St. Marychurch Road. Bear right, past the Mormon church on your right and cross to reach the edge of Milber Pine Woods indicating the beginning of the Pine Walk through the woods.

Milber Pine Woods actually comprises mixed coniferous and deciduous and there are many large, mature beech trees growing along the sides of the straight Pine Walk.

A gradual ascent brings you almost level with St. Marychurch Road where you enter 'Ben Stedham's Wood' which is here marked by a commemorative plaque erected by Newton Abbot Urban District Council in 1968. You should bear slightly to the right and follow the path, along the right hand side of the wood.

You are quite likely to spot some grey squirrels as you cross the springy turf in the cool shade of the wood.

You reach Milber Lane at the top of the wood. Turn right and continue along a level and well used path which is actually a bridleway flanked by gorse, brambles, scrub oak and, in summer, much rose bay willow herb. Unfortunately, you have not long to enjoy this old way – a great chunk has been taken out of it by the extension of Aller Vale quarry back into the hillside.

Look out for a stile on the left where the farmer has allowed a diversion across his field to substitute for the route along Milber Lane. (If you pass this you will soon find the way barred and a notice DANGER - QUARRY WORKINGS ahead.) Cross this stile and follow the hedgerow on your right to reach the gravelly track which runs parallel to Milber Lane. Turn right and follow the track until it veers right to merge into the old way again.

On your left are the flanks of Milber Down Camp, an Iron Age fort which was later used by the Romans. Across Aller Vale, along which runs the railway line and main road to Torquay, can be seen the village of Abbotskerswell nestling amid a fold in the hills. There too is St. Augustine's Priory which, from this angle, appears to overlook Abbotskerswell.

Past Haccombe Farm the path becomes a metalled track and you begin to descend towards the valley in which the village of Coffinswell is situated. At the road junction you turn left and continue through the village, most of whose dwellings flank the road and provide interesting viewing.

The houses and gardens are all quite immaculate; strange that there never seem to be any people about here! At the Old Well House there is a well, or spring, on the grass verge by the roadside. A stream of water passes under the road and runs through a delightful garden opposite.

Continue through the village until the junction at The Linny Free House is reached. To leave Coffinswell you take the lane behind

The Linny, shown as Ridgeway Lane on the Pathfinder map, but first you may care to look at the church and what is indicated on the same map as 'Court Barton'. To do so you turn right at The Linny and then left between outbuildings of Court Barton Farm.

A massive granite arch stands before the yard of the farmhouse. The older part of the building on the right dates from the sixteenth century and contains some mullioned windows of granite. Unfortunately, for security's sake, St. Bartholomew's, the thirteenth century parish church, is kept locked, but you can see quite a lot by peering through the windows. The interior appears to be relatively plain and simple and unVictorianised; the absence of a screen and the Norman font of Beer stone are especially striking.

Barton Gate, Coffinswell, before recent partial rebuilding

The next stage of this ramble takes you uphill by the lane behind The Linny to reach St. Marychurch Road. Here you have reached an altitude of 150 metres and it is worth pausing to take in the view, particularly the panorama to the south-west – the Torbay hinterland. Turn right and sharp left along a track which soon becomes sunken, overhung with branches, and dark as a result.

The track is signposted as Deerpark Lane; no doubt the deerpark referred to was that of Haccombe House, about a kilometre to the north (left) and just visible at one point.

You emerge at a lane known as Ridge Road where, straight ahead, there is a surprising view of the sea through a cleft in the hills behind Babbacombe Bay. Turn left here and follow this lane, very little used by motor traffic, for about a mile.

There are extremely few signs of human habitation and an area about half way along here is aptly named 'No Man's Land'. You will enjoy some fine views across the estuary towards Bishopsteignton, Teignmouth and the sweep of the East Devon coast and inland towards Dartmoor.

You reach a junction marked by a clearing in which grows a large ash tree – a sort of green mini-roundabout. Here you leave the road and bear right along a track, passing a small copse on your right. Soon after you begin the descent to Combeinteignhead look out for a narrow path on the right which descends more steeply and is well sunken, with trees meeting overhead. At a junction of tracks, head straight across to continue the descent. When you reach the lane bear left through the village. Conveniently sited for your refreshment is the Wild Goose Free House.

Just past the pub look out for the lych gate to the parish church which is well worth a visit but first notice the old Church House to your right. Built of the local red conglomerate rock, the structure provides a contrast to the grey limestone of Coffinswell. A plaque on the wall reads as follows:

> *This building was erected
> and presented to the Parish
> as an Almshouse by
> William Bourchier
> 3rd Earl of Bath
> A.D. 1620*

A leaflet on the church and parish of Combeinteignhead explains that this building originally served as a Church House, upstairs being used for harvest suppers and village functions while downstairs was let as a tavern. Not until the end of the eighteenth century was the ground floor used to house two poor families, hence 'Bourchier's Almshouse', while the first floor became the village school.

Bourchier's Almshouses, Combeinteignhead

Now to the parish church: Handsome sandstone pillars either side of the nave give access to the aisles which lead up to hagioscopes with glass panes. These and a heavy thirteenth century screen serve to render the chancel somewhat hidden and dark, in contrast to the light and airy feeling which pervades the rest of the church.

> Leave the churchyard by a gate opposite the porch and proceed by a grassy track to reach the road where you bear left. Turn left at the junction with Shaldon Road towards Newton Abbot. After a short distance, take the right fork for Lower Netherton.

An initial climb is rewarded by some delightful views over the cluster of fields, orchards and farms which comprise Lower Netherton. Some of the buildings around here appear to be quite ancient. In contrast with this march the serried ranks of bungalows at Buckland on the crest of the hill ahead.

> Follow the lane down between the farms and keep to the right as you begin to climb. This straight, ascending road will lead you to Hackney Lane where you turn right and descend to the Teign estuary where, providing the tide is not too high, you can make your way back to Newton Abbot by the footpath along the banks of the estuary and Rivers Teign and Lemon. You must divert briefly away from the river at Forde Road and then regain it at Newton Abbot Quay. Go under the railway and turn left into Teign Road, past Tuckers Maltings and bear right via Quay Road to meet Queen Street and reach the station.

Gleanings

The origins of the place names encountered on this ramble prove to be of some interest. Gover's *Place Names of Devon* explains that *Milber* is derived from 'Milbourne' or mill-stream, the mills in question being the old Aller Mill and Keyberry Mill, reputed to date back to Saxon times.

Coffinswell was once known simply as 'Well' but was so called after Hugo Coffin who was Lord of the Manor in the twelfth century.

Combeinteignhead is a nineteenth century corruption of 'Combe-in-ten-hydes' and has nothing to do with the River Teign. The village was situated in an outlier of Wonford Hundred which measured ten hydes in extent.

Netherton means 'nether-ton' or lower-farm and distinguished a lower farm in relation to Haccombe; Lower Netherton is therefore literally 'lower-lower-farm'.

Lower Netherton

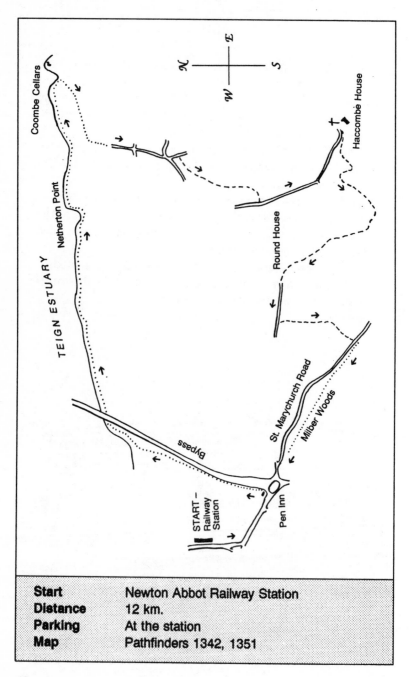

Start	Newton Abbot Railway Station
Distance	12 km.
Parking	At the station
Map	Pathfinders 1342, 1351

7
NEWTON ABBOT CIRCULAR
via Teign Estuary, Haccombe and Milber

Going: The path along the bank of the estuary is normally flooded and therefore impassable at high tide, so it is advisable to check tide times before setting out. You should avoid this section of the route within an hour either side of high water. The route after Coombe Cellars is easy walking and should present few problems.

From Newton Abbot Railway Station bear left towards the Torquay Road. Cross the railway and walk past Forde House, the handsome Elizabethan mansion recently restored and now occupied by Teignbridge District Council. At the Pen Inn leave the pavement and walk across the forecourt of the pub towards a Public Footpath sign in the right hand corner.

This is a newly created right of way (it does not appear on the current Pathfinder map) which offers a direct and amenable approach to the River Teign. The path runs parallel and close to the Newton Abbot - Kingsteignton bypass but, because it runs at a slightly lower level than the road, much of the noise passes over one's head. On the other side of the path flows the Aller Brook which meets the Teign.

Bear right, on reaching the confluence, and simply follow the riverside, or estuary-side path, now signposted the Templer Way.

Across the river is low lying land covered with rushes and intersected by a number of creeks and channels. Beyond that you will see the tower of Kingsteignton church and a number of railway wagons and coaches in Hackney sidings.

|| Continue along the riverside footpath towards the bypass flyover.

The marine influence in the estuary is indicated by the bladder-wrack attached to the stone banks of the river here. Before you make your way under the flyover (how much quieter it must have been before) you will see on the far bank the ruins of the hamlet of Hackney dwarfed by the vast span of the new concrete bridge. On the far side of the flyover you will see the Passage House Inn and massive new hotel and the village of Bishopsteignton further along.

The Teign estuary now opens up before you; either a sheet of (usually) calm water or an expanse of mud, depending upon the state of the tide. The reedy islands opposite are a good place to spot herons, whilst the tiny islets in mid-estuary seem to be a stronghold of cormorants. The herons actually nest further along the estuary in the woods around Netherton House.

As you progress along the shore you are made more aware of the varied bird life of the estuary. One still, misty day in early September practically the only sound and sight of movement were the plops of terns as they dived down into the shallow water after fish. They would alight from the water almost immediately and continue their reconnaissance from the air. Their method of flying and appearance in flight reminded me how apt is their alternative name of sea swallow. One morning during another September I saw a solitary redshank and lapwing and a pair of oystercatchers.

You may notice that around Wildlands Point and Buckland Point you are passing over a hard, massive rock which outcrops on the banks of the estuary. This is dolerite, an intrusive, igneous rock. Further along towards Netherton Point there is an outcrop of Devonian slate and the ground becomes softer where it is composed of a mass of tiny fragments of slate derived from the bedrock.

|| Once past the woods which mark the site of Netherton House you follow the estuary bank until you encounter a number of shacks and a view of Coombe Cellars pub with its landing stage.

The landing stage is where boats from Teignmouth moor at high tide during the summer to disgorge thirsty holidaymakers. You may wish to visit the pub in which case you will have to mount the stone wall by the steps provided in order to cross the brook which discharges into the estuary at this inlet.

It is possible to continue walking along the estuary bank for about another kilometre as far as Arch Brook Bridge but the route of this ramble entails turning inland just before Coombe Cellars by the path which starts at the stile by the steps opposite the pub which is indicated by a Public Footpath sign. Once over the stile you head diagonally across the field towards a gap in the hedge in the opposite corner, then follow the hedge on your left as far as the edge of Netherton Woods to pass through a gate in the far right hand corner where you will find a lane leading to your left away from Netherton House. Follow this lane over a crossroads and by Cross Park, a row of six rustic style council houses with delightful gardens.

Haccombe House

Once past Cross Park you emerge onto the Shaldon Road where you turn right and sharp left into Ridge Road and then sharp right along an unmetalled track which descends gradually among the scattered farms and cottages of Higher Netherton.

The vale of Haccombe gradually unfolds before you. Pine woods crown the crest of the hill on the far side. You will notice how deep red is the colour of the soil along this track as you cross a brook and begin to ascend slightly to the road.

Turn left at the road and walk along the straight route towards Home Farm. The fields here are not protected from the road by hedges or stone walls but by wire strung to posts which indicates a modern origin. Home Farm has a Victorian appearance and I would guess that the farm was created out of the former parkland of Haccombe House comparatively recently. When you reach Home Farm you pass through a pair of massive granite gate posts and make your way along the drive towards Haccombe House, now in full view.

An avenue of fine trees once led to Haccombe House which is described by Sabine Baring-Gould as a 'hideous structure'; even W.G. Hoskins describes it as 'plain'. It is a late Georgian pile of about 1805 and reminds me of the manor house at West Ogwell which dates from the same period. Hoskins tells us that Haccombe manor belonged to the Haccombes in the twelfth and thirteenth centuries, passed to the Courtenays and then by marriage to the Carews who held it from the mid-fifteenth century.

Haccombe Church, which stands beside the house, is dedicated to St. Blaize and mostly dates from the thirteenth century. It is reputed to contain some fine brasses and effigies but the opportunity to view the interior of the church does not arise as it appears to be kept permanently locked, apart from occasional services. Outside can be seen several graves of members of the Carew family. The house now is split up into flats.

With your back to Haccombe House, take the track which leads away to the left. This track climbs up the south side of Haccombe

St. Blaize's Church, Haccombe

vale and winds its way towards Wren Cottage and affords more good views back across Haccombe Vale.

Continue past Wren Cottage to enter the woods, and keep climbing along a path lined with rhododendrons and through woods consisting mainly of pine trees and silver birch.

The soil here is not the deep red colour that it is in the valley; it is instead grey. This variation is enough to indicate a different geological formation. Here you are passing over the sands and gravels of the Cretaceous Period and the resultant acid soil is fit only for the pine woods and heath which cover much of Milber Down.

Keep to the main path until you emerge at a high point beside the Round House, from where you begin your descent to Newton Abbot. Carry on in the same general direction. Once past the works on your left look out for a dirt track which turns off left between the works and house gardens on your right. Follow this lane, cross Chestnut Drive (not shown on the Ordnance Survey map) and continue by the track on the far side. Cross St. Marychurch Road and turn right for the footpath through Milber Pine Woods which offers a pleasant and safe descent to Pennin from where, via the subway to the pub, you can retrace your steps to the railway station.

Iron Gate at Haccombe

Gleanings

Teign Estuary: The scene at sunset on spring-tides is of magnificent grandeur. The many-hued water, with perchance a barge or sail in the foreground; Kingsteignton and Newton in the middle distance; and beyond, the Dartmoor hills bathed in a glorious soft wealth of colour — such a sense as neither pencil nor brush can adequately describe.

Coombe Cellars: Pleasantly situated on the river, is noted for cockles, Devonshire cream, etc., and is much frequented in the summer by visitors from Teignmouth and Newton Abbot ... Here we may play skittles or quoits till tea time, or just sit still and enjoy the sea breeze, or hire a boat and spend an hour on the water. The cockle teas here really should be tried.
Talks on Walks in and around Newton Abbot, c. 1915

A well-known spot on the Teign is **Coombe Cellars**, near Combe-in-Teignhead, which consists of an inn built on a spit of land jutting out into the river, and reached by a causeway. From the balcony of the hostel a magnificent view is seen of the estuary, with the hills of Dartmoor in the distance. The house, which has been a place of call for boating-parties for about a century, was originally thatched with its walls decorated all over with cockleshells, reminiscent of the standing dish served at the inn. The house was partly rebuilt a few years ago, when a modern roofing was substituted for the comelier thatch.
Sidney Heath: *The South Devon and Dorset Coast,* 1910

> *For there's Bishop's teign*
> *And King's teign*
> *And Coomb at the clear teign head —*
> *Where close by the stream*
> *You may have your cream*
> *All spread upon barley bread.*
>
> John Keats, 1818

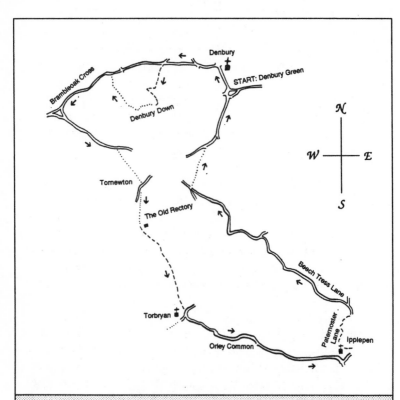

Start	Denbury village
Distance	10 km., longer with possible diversions
Getting there	From Newton Abbot, take the Totnes Road and turn right, either past Wolborough Cemetery or at the Tow Mile Oak Inn.
Parking	As you approach from the Two Mile Oak, there is an extensive layby just past the village green, opposite the high wall and before the village centre.
Bus	There is no bus service to Denbury. You could take bus No. 75 from Newton Abbot to Ipplepen and make that village your starting and finishing point.
Map	Pathfinder 1351
Reference	824688

8
DENBURY CIRCULAR
via Torbryan and Ipplepen

Going: Not over-strenuous and a delightful walk with many points of interest. Denbury is an attractive village, neither swamped with new housing nor too precious. The church must be visited. Denbury Down is newly accessible to the public, courtesy of Devon County Council. Torbryan Church is another gem and, though declared redundant, is undergoing restoration. Orley Common is a nature reserve under the auspices of Teignbridge District Council.

Walk towards the village crossroads – notice the church tower looming on the right, as if the church did not want to miss out on any of the village goings-on.

Denbury parish church, St. Mary, has a cruciform layout and the entire structure dates from the early fourteenth century. The interior of the church has some striking features. There are massive blue and purple-streaked limestone slabs on the floor of the nave, a fine Norman font of red sandstone, whitewashed walls, a splendid barrel-vaulted ceiling and an organ loft in the tower overhead. The vestry screen has recently been constructed from timber salvaged from the pews of St. Mary, Abbotsbury – it's heartening to see a church so well cared for and still being improved. The absence of altar rail or screen affords an almost unimpeded view from the pews to the altar. The list of rectors dates from 1278, which was eight years before Denbury was granted a market. In the following century it became a borough but never actually grew beyond a village.

Denbury Church

Back at the crossroads you go straight across to West Street, sign-posted to Ashburton and Woodland, past Gaia House, the New Age Centre, then take the left fork – Woodlands Road. Just past and opposite the last bungalow take the unmade track leading uphill towards Denbury Down. The track makes a dog-leg bend to cope with the rise, then reaches a gate by which you enter the wooded summit.

The wooded hill and two adjoining fields have recently been acquired by Devon County Council which is maintaining the area as a nature reserve. Steps and a stile have been installed and a walk through this elevated deciduous natural woodland, never dark but well lit and with a wealth of wild flora and birdlife, is a delight.

Follow the track through the wood – if you keep to the main track you won't go wrong. As you begin to descend the track bifurcates – head straight down by the wooden steps to reach a stile at the edge of the wood. Climb over and follow the hedgerow to reach the lane.

Denbury Down is an unmistakable landmark in this region. It owes its existence to a capping of basalt, a hard volcanic rock which protects the limestone which it intrudes. The origin of the name Denbury means 'the fort of the men of Devon' and, as Hoskins points out, may well commemorate a stronghold where the original Celtic inhabitants of this land held out for a time against a Saxon advance from the Teign estuary. It is likely, however, that the defensive earthworks on Denbury Down date back to much earlier times, to 300 B.C. according to one authority.

Denbury village

Just before the junction (given on the Pathfinder map as Yeatt Cross but indicated on the ground as Brambleoak Cross) it is possible to cut off the corner by following an enclosed path on the left. When I came this way in May 1992 it was passable but only with difficulty. The shrubs – actually bramble oak – were growing vigorously across the path from either side.

Now on the south side of Denbury Down follow the lane, but look out for a Public Footpath sign on your right. Cross the stile and head across the field towards a second stile in the wire fence.

The Pathfinder map shows the right of way here has been rerouted to avoid the farm buildings by passing to their left. Carry on to reach the lane and bear right.

Look out for a stone slab stile and Public Footpath sign on your left. Cross here and follow the beaten path to drop down to reach the track below, just before the house. Walk past the former Rectory, a rather magnificent residence overlooking a water garden, and follow the track ahead.

The thick woods in the valley obscure the many caves, quarries and kilns which the Pathfinder map indicates in this limestone country. The bones of many extinct mammals have been uncovered in the caves hereabouts, a location contemporary with Kent's Cavern at Torquay.

At the first gate the tower of Torbryan Church comes into view. The elaborate iron gate at the end leads you into the village, or hamlet, of Torbryan.

Here there is a splendid church and a wonderful old pub, both worth exploring for different kinds of refreshment. Holy Trinity Church is now maintained under the Redundant Churches Fund and is currently undergoing repairs. An interesting potted history and plan of the structure is posted just inside the church. The interior is very light, intensely peaceful and beautified by a magnificent fifteenth century screen decorated with figure paintings.

Before leaving Torbryan, if you have time, you should continue up the lane past the Church House Inn. This leads through a gate into a field; follow the wall on the left until you reach the brow of the hill. From here you have a good view towards the southwest across some unspoilt country. You can see the village of Broadhempston and some southerly peaks of Dartmoor. If you descend to the bottom of the field you can cross a stile and enter a charming water meadow through which runs Am Brook.

Several leats are cut here which, in a wet season, brim with flowing water. When I visited the meadow one July I found the leats quite dried up and only Am Brook giving sustenance to Great Willow Herb,

Meadowsweet, Scarce Willow Herb and Marsh Woundwort, in addition to many colourful dragonflies.

Climbing the hill to return to Torbryan, it is curious to find the top of the lofty church tower coming into view. At the summit you are only about a hundred metres distant from the tower but almost at the same altitude as its crowning pinnacles.

Torbryan Church

At the junction in Torbryan you turn right towards Ipplepen. Follow the lane as it climbs up towards Orley Common. The Common presents another possible diversion, and surely one not to be missed. There are some enjoyable views back towards Torbryan whose church and pub and few cottages seem to nestle in a hollow in the hills.

Orley Common is a wooded hillside managed by Teignbridge District Council which has provided a car park and information boards detailing its paths and special features. If you follow the main track away from the lane you will reach the heath-like summit where bracken, brambles and wild roses are surrounded by common woodland trees such as oak and ash. The open top is traversed by deeply rutted tracks in which can be seen great chunks of grey limestone.

Along the borders of these tracks grows a wealth of wild flowers. Among those I managed to identify one July day are many which, according to Keble Martin, are lovers of dry or calcareous soils, which certainly corresponds to this location. These included St. John's Wort, Lady's Bedstraw, Restharrow, Musk or Nodding Thistle, Spear Thistle, Meadow Clary, Field Scabious and Greater Knapweed. Among the butterflies enjoying this variety of flowering plants were the Marbled White and Small Tortoiseshell species.

Back on the road turn right towards Ipplepen. As you proceed along Silver Street you should look for a gate on the left which leads into the churchyard.

If you feel inclined to inspect a third church in one day you should take a look inside Ipplepen Church and purchase a copy of the interesting booklet *The Churches and Parishes of Ipplepen and Torbryan*, written by a former vicar of Ipplepen. This informs the reader that, though the present church dates from the fourteenth and fifteenth centuries, it was preceded by a Norman church and, before that, by a Saxon Church, Ipplepen being the mother parish of an extensive Deanery.

In the churchyard you should look for a stile in the wall opposite the gate by which you first entered the churchyard. This leads into Paternoster Lane where you turn left (but turn right to reach the village pub) and follow the narrow winding lane which effectively bypasses the village, described by Hoskins himself as 'grey' and 'rather dismal'. There is certainly much modern development which tends to submerge the old village at the centre.

Paternoster Lane reaches a T-junction where you should bear left and then fork left down Beech Trees Lane.

You are soon back in deep country. Follow this quiet lane as it rises gradually then descends steeply, crosses a stream and rises once more. Now look out for a stile and Public Footpath sign on your right. Enter the field here and head towards the gate in the hedgebank opposite, then to the right of a barn to reach the lane. Bear right to reach Denbury. Perhaps a stop at the Union Inn on Denbury Green will slake the thirst developed on this final stretch.

Gleanings

The most remarkable district fair was that of **Denbury**, which came to a close by operation of the rinderpest in 1866, after continuing from 1285, when it was granted to the Abbot of Tavistock. It was held on the 19th of September, and was attended by all classes. The carriages of the county families of the district were to be seen there; it became the fixed day for the payment of rents; and it was in many ways the pivot on which the business and pleasure of the twelve months turned. Strangely, however, Denbury Fair, under the old name, kept in the old way, yet thrives in Labrador, established three generations since by Devonshire settlers, and still dear to their descendants, though these are quite ignorant whether Denbury be the name of man, woman, place, or thing.
R.N. Worth: *A History of Devonshire*, 1886

Torbryan takes its name from the rocky land and tors around it. The whole parish abounds in wild but beautiful scenery, and the eye rests with delight on the church, as its tower rises from the dark wood in which it is embosomed.
Octavian Blewitt: *The Panorama of Torquay*, 1832

Ipplepen is a respectable village, situated about three miles south-west of Newton. At an angular point in the centre of the village, stands part of the ancient cross, from which some uncommonly interesting views of Denbury-down and the adjacent eminences are commanded.
Rev. D.M. Stirling: *A History of Newton-Abbot and Newton-Bushel*, 1830

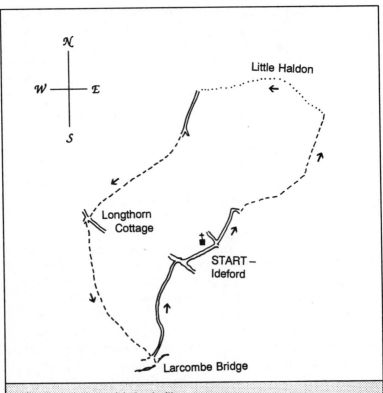

Start	Ideford village
Distance	5 km.
Getting there	From Newton Abbot take the Kingsteignton Road. Drive through the village main street and, at the junction, turn right along the lane signposted to Ideford and Luton. This will take you over the bypass and lead you by a winding way to a junction midway between the sister villages of Ideford and Luton — Ideford is to the left.
Parking	There is usually space to park on the lane beside the church.
Bus	X46, X47
Map	Pathfinder 1342
Reference	895775

9
IDEFORD CIRCULAR
via Little Haldon

Going: This route reaches the highest altitude of any of the rambles in this book: around 215 metres That is a rise of around 115 metres from Ideford Church, which itself is around 30 metres above the low point of the walk at Larcombe Bridge. This entails a good steady climb at the beginning of the walk, but the way is never uncomfortably steep.

The panoramic views enjoyed from Little Haldon probably surpass any described in this book.

From Ideford Church walk uphill, away from the village centre, over the crossroads and up Butts Lane. Pass the lone modern house on your left and continue to climb by the enclosed path up the flank of Little Haldon. Eventually the arable fields cease and uncultivated common land begins.

At the end of the enclosed path bear half left and follow the beaten path through the heather and gorse and pines. Keep heading in the same general direction, north-westwards, with tremendous views back across Ideford and Luton and in all directions south, east and west.

A more significant track joins from the right. Carry on until you walk through the gypsy settlement.

You will no doubt set off the barking of many dogs, but you are more likely to see horses, donkeys, cats, hens and ducks.

Follow the metalled lane, ignore the Bridleway to the left and continue downhill, with a wood on your right. Soon the path forks

– the lane heads left and directly to Ideford. Carry straight on by the stony enclosed track. This will carry you to Longthorn Cottage. Cross the road and take the similar stony track opposite – half left between the two surfaced lanes. This way rises slightly and then descends steeply to a barn just above the ford and pedestrian only Larcombe Bridge.

Larcombe Bridge

This footbridge is known as Larcombe Bridge. Larcombe is derived from the Saxon and means 'the valley where wild iris grows'.

Turn left here to climb steadily past Town Farm and into Ideford village. The Royal Oak – a pub worth veturing into – greets you at the crossroads.

Alternative linear walk to National Trust car park on Little Haldon

Going: You will have to arrange to be picked up at either end of this walk. Apart from the initial descent to Larcombe Bridge, the going is uphill all the way – you know you've had a walk by the end of it, and you do get the sense of having climbed a substantial hill. If you want a really lazy alternative, you could of course do the walk the other way round, i.e. begin on Little Haldon and descend all the way to Larcombe Bridge, then tackle the gentle ascent to the centre of Ideford.

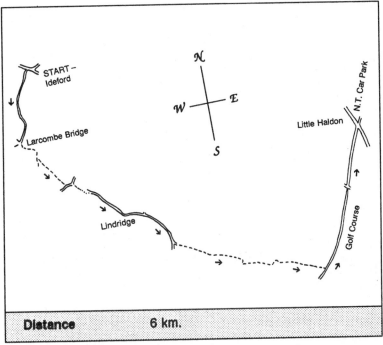

Distance   6 km.

At Ideford you take the minor road opposite the pub which leads in a southerly direction past Town Farm. You descend to a crossroads where you turn left across a stone footbridge.

Follow the track and make a gradual ascent. After following a right hand bend you reach a fork where you bear left. Continue to ascend up the hedge-lined, flint-strewn track. When you reach a metalled lane turn left.

At this junction there is a terrific view back across Ideford to the pine-clad ridge of Great Haldon and, to the right, across Ideford's sister village of Luton to the heather-clad summit of Little Haldon.

About 25 metres down the lane on your right is the entrance to a narrow enclosed path which cuts off a corner on our route. Bear left where it meets the lane, past the entrance to Lindridge Park.

The entrance gateway is quite impressive. Granite-topped, red sandstone gateposts lead to an avenue of trees; the old gatehouse to the left is known as 'Avenue House'. Lindridge House was one of the old manor houses of Bishopsteignton and burnt down a few years ago.

Further on the road forks. The main road bears to the right but you bear left up a track signposted as 'Unsuitable for Motors'. The going becomes a little strenuous as you make a direct ascent up the western slope of Little Haldon.

Perhaps you will pause and take in the view northwards over the countryside. The fields are quite a bit larger than one grows to expect in South Devon. They are also uncharacteristically straight-edged. The sight of these fields, as they sweep up the flanks of Little Haldon, reminds one more of the sweeping downland of Wiltshire than the more higgledy-piggledy countryside of South Devon.

As you continue to climb you pass through two right angles, first right, then left. First the track enters coniferous woods, then crosses heathland to emerge at a T-junction with the road over Little Haldon.

You are now at an altitude of about 235 metres. The highest point is actually 237 metres but this is somewhere on the Golf Course opposite and is not apparent from the road across the plateau-like summit.

Turn left here and continue in a northerly direction.

On the left hand side, the west facing slope of Little Haldon is characterised by a flora of heather and gorse. The area on your right hand, occupied by Teignmouth Golf Course, is predominantly grass with patches of heath to provide a place where inaccurate golfers lose their balls. Teignmouth Golf Course is sited on the former Haldon Aerodrome, originally opened in 1929 to offer flying lessons. In the 1930s the GWR (yes, the Great Western Railway) began a regular air service, twice daily, flying between Haldon, Cardiff and Plymouth. The aerodrome was converted to military use during World War 2 and closed down soon after the cessation of hostilities.

|| Follow the lane to reach the junction with the Exeter - Teignmouth
|| road. On the opposite side is a large National Trust car park.

In the far corner of the car park is a toposcope to help you pinpoint various landmarks. The view from the road is panoramic, to say the least. There is Newton Abbot to the south-west, Bovey Tracey and Haytor to the west, Chudleigh and the lake at Ugbrooke to the north-west and forested Great Haldon to the north. In a north-easterly direction you will be thrilled to see the beautiful coastline of East Devon and West Dorset. It is usually possible to see the red cliffs of Exmouth but when the visibility is good you can decipher the white chalk cliffs at Beer Head, Golden Cap in Dorset (the highest point on the south coast) and, on exceptionally clear days, the unmistakable wedge of Portland, the eastern extremity of Lyme Bay and some 47 miles distant!

It is inevitably cooler at this altitude and there always seems to be a westerly wind gusting up the slopes here, Haldon being the first obstacle to the prevailing westerlies from Dartmoor.

When you see the topsoil here, you will notice that it contains many whitish flints. These flints represent the insoluble residue from a stratum of chalk which once covered the Haldon Hills.

Ideford Church

The exterior of Ideford Church is mainly of red sandstone which was extracted from the old quarry at Ideford Arch. Closer examination of the walls reveals pieces of conglomerate, granite, limestone and greenstone. Whilst looking at the outside you may notice an ancient carved tympanum, or door-lintel, fixed into the external wall of the chancel. This carving depicts a dragon and bird and dates from 1050-1100. It was found under the present chancel during restoration work and seems to indicate the existence of a Norman church on this site.

The present church dates from the thirteenth to fifteenth centuries. Inside you can see parts of a fifteenth century screen which have been incorporated into the pulpit and two sanctuary chairs.

An old stone slab stile, this one near Tornewton, see Walk 8

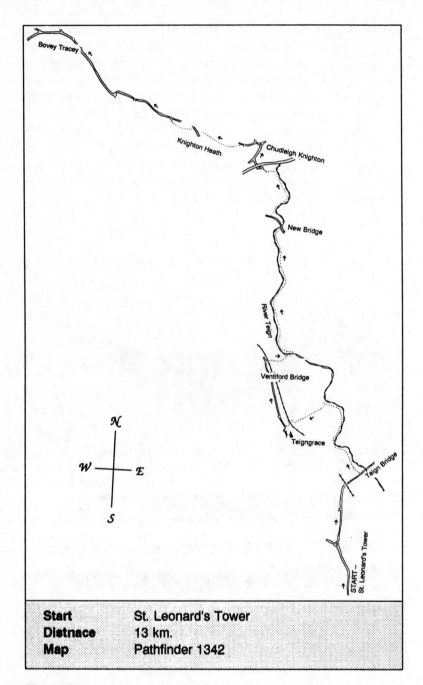

Bovey Tracey

Knighton Heath

Chudleigh Knighton

New Bridge

River Teign

Ventiford Bridge

Teigngrace

Teign Bridge

START –
St. Leonard's Tower

N
W — E
S

Start	St. Leonard's Tower
Distnace	13 km.
Map	Pathfinder 1342

10

NEWTON ABBOT - BOVEY TRACEY

via Teign Bridge, Teigngrace and Chudleigh Knighton

Going: This is a ramble particularly for those with a penchant for transport and industry. The main interest of this walk lies in the evidence of man's efforts today and in the past to extract clay and move goods, although there is much of interest to the naturalist in the varied habitat of filed, marsh, riverside, heath and industrial wasteland.

The route of this ramble takes you through the low-lying Bovey Basin from Teign Bridge at the southern end to Bovey Tracey in the north. Much of this land is excavated and mined for ball clay, and much of the remainder is used as a dump for the rejected materials dug in the process. What remains of the basin is heath as at Knighton and Bovey Heaths or arable land on the flood plains of the Rivers Teign and Bovey. The walking is level but muddy in wet weather.

From St. Leonard's Tower walk up Bank Street, Highweek Street and, at the roundabout with the Ashburton Road, head straight on along the Bovey Road. There is a pavement from the roundabout at the junction with the Ashburton Road which takes you past Jetty Marsh Lane, the Churchills Estate, the entrance to Sandford Orleigh and the Church Path to All Saints. Unfortunately, at this point the pavement ends but you have only to descend a further 200 metres or so to reach the crossroads just past Whitehill Garage, but do take care. Here you take a right turn away from the busy main road and by the fields towards Teign Bridge.

As you approach the turning for Teigngrace the road becomes a sort of causeway as it rises above the many channels which crisscross the marshy, low-lying fields in the vicinity.

|| Soon you reach a level crossing and a bridge.

The level crossing takes you over the former Moretonhampstead Branch Line which still runs as far as Heathfield where it serves a number of plants on the industrial estate there. Looking south from the level crossing you can see a couple of sidings with heavy-duty ramps on which clay lorries can empty their contents into waiting railway wagons.

Bridge over Stover Canal, near Teign Bridge

Adjacent to the level crossing is a bridge spanning the former Stover Canal, unused since before the Second World War, but once used by barges carrying ball clay and granite through the Bovey Basin and down the Teign estuary to the port of Teignmouth. The buildings which line the canal bank on the left as you look south from the bridge are former clay cellars, as is the single storey building with heavily buttressed walls just below the bridge on your right. What a scene of toil it must have been in the days when men spiked the 35lb 'balls' of clay and carried them from the clay cellars to the waiting barges!

As you continue towards Teign Bridge look for a stile on the left which leads you down to a riverside path, through what are commonly known as Teign Fields.

Before you leave the road it is worth taking a look back towards the hills to the south which lie in a line between Bovey and Ashburton Roads. Highweek Hill is to the left and is distinguished by the tower of All Saints Church, Gaze Hill is in the middle and Darracombe Beacon is the conical hill on the right. Much further away to the north-west is the unmistakeable peak of Haytor.

You now follow the well-beaten riverside footpath.

These low-lying fields form the flood plain of the lower Teign and are, indeed, often flooded after heavy rainfall on the moors has swollen the waters of the Teign.

All the apparent hills in the vicinity are man-made from the unwanted material excavated from the many clay pits and mines which have been dug in the Bovey Basin. Many of them have been landscaped but continue to look profoundly unnatural as their regularly pitched slopes rise abruptly from an otherwise flat countryside to uniformly flat summits. Perhaps it would be more interesting to have the weird white pyramids of St. Austell.

Look out for a signpost beside the path. This indicates the riverside path in either direction and a course to the left through fields towards Teigngrace. Follow this latter route to enjoy an interesting diversion via Teigngrace and Ventiford Bridge. Alternatively, you could continue by the riverside path to reach a footbridge across the river.

To follow the way to Teigngrace: look for a wooden stile in the hedge on the left hand side of the field and head towards it. Continue across the next field and cross the far boundary by way of a narrow footbridge which carries you over a double-ditched hedgebank. Crossing the next field you will see the tower of Teigngrace Church come into view as you approach a five-bar gate opposite. Once through this gate the path becomes a track which runs over a footbridge made of old railway sleepers, then bears right before the ditch ahead which is all that remains of the Stover Canal.

As you mount the bridge over the canal you will see to your right an impressive wall built of massive granite blocks with recesses on each side which once housed a pair of lock gates. It is worth following the canal bank on the right to find the other pair of lock gates further upstream. The two sets of gates are 110 feet apart which was sufficient to take two barges at a time. The wooden gates at the upstream point are more of less intact and it is tempting to imagine the scene here in the canal's more active days.

On the far side of the canal runs the railway track, and just beyond the second pair of lack gates you can see the little platform of the former Teigngrace Halt.

You will probably also want to visit the church at Teigngrace (it is usually locked but the key is obtainable nearby). It was built on the site of an earlier church in 1787 by the Templers of Stover who were also responsible for building the canal, in 1792, and for the construction of the Haytor Granite Tramway, in 1820. Teigngrace Church is certainly quite unlike any other church visited in the course of these rambles. Hoskins describes it as 'an early specimen of Strawberry Hill Gothic' and I would certainly endorse the description in White's 1850 Directory of Devon which says of Teigngrace Church that 'the interior has more the appearance of an elegant domestic chapel than that of a parish church', so full of memorials to the Templer family is it.

From Teigngrace you make your way north along the lane to Ventiford Bridge, the terminal basin of the Stover Canal.

It is possible to distinguish fragments of the stone walls which enclosed the circular basin where barges were turned round to be reloaded. The Haytor Granite Tramway ended here after its seven-mile descent from the quarries at Haytor. On the edge of the basin can be seen the broken shaft and toothed iron wheel of an old crane. Ventiford was also a centre for barge building.

> From Ventiford Bridge follow the path by the brook over a wooden stile to the confluence of the brook with the Teign. Turn right to follow the river downstream until you reach the recently built footbridge across the River Teign. Cross here and bear left to follow the riverside path upstream, past the confluence of the River Bovey, clay pits to your right, until you reach New Bridge.

One day in late October 1979, I was startled to see a huge fish suddenly leap out of the water. It was all of three feet long: a salmon, I presumed. I wonder if such large salmon are still to be seen in the Teign?

New Bridge, near Chudleigh Knighton

Beyond New Bridge Ball Clay Works, opposite the entrance to E.C.C. New Bridge Works and Twinyeo (= 'between the waters': Rivers Bovey and Teign) Farm you cross a wooden stile along an indicated Public Bridleway through a wood.

This soon brings you back to the River Teign which you follow until you almost reach the A38. The path then bears left, away from the river and heads through woodland to meet a track – turn right here to reach a gate – now follow the metalled road under the dual carriageway to Chudleigh Knighton.When you reach the old Plymouth Road turn right towards the church.

The church, as you can see, is built of limestone and flint. The flint is reminiscent of the chalk country of south-seat England and is most unusually found as a building stone in South Devon. Flint is found locally on the summits of the nearby Haldon Hills.Chudleigh Knighton church is a chapel-of-ease built in the early English style in 1841-2.

Flint and limestone at Chudleigh Knighton Church

|| Turn left at the church.

You may notice a tablet set high in the wall of a cottage on the right at the junction ahead. It reads as follows:

> THIS IS GOD'S COM
> MANDMENT that we
> should believe on
> the name of his son
> JESUS CHRIST
> and love one another

Bear left at this junction, past the thatched Clay Cutters Arms pub, along the road towards Bovey Tracey. Just beyond the children's playground on the edge of the village you will find the beginning of a tarmacced path by which you can avoid the road for half a mile or so and feel a closer contact with the character of Knighton Heath through which you are walking.

The most characteristic vegetation here seems to be gorse and brambles, heather and a variety of grasses; the most common tree the silver birch. The Hennock massif rises majestically out of the plain on your right whilst ahead is Haytor.

The footpath emerges onto a road where you turn right towards Dunley Cross. Just before you reach the road look out for the start of another footpath on the left which allows you to follow a course away from but parallel to the road. Once again you emerge at the road and there is now little choice but to follow the road to Bovey Tracey. You do pass several parcels of land on the left which contain former clay pits, now flooded and managed as nature reserves. There is access to these and it is possible to leave the road from time to time to enter them. Some are still in a state of development and access should improve. as time goes by.

The stone walls which begin to appear as you approach the church exhibit a dazzling variety of rock types. There is granite and limestone but also various volcanic rocks and chunks of veined gneiss.

Bovey Tracey Church is well worth a visit. Its tower is untypically (for a Devon Church) tall and slender. The interior is curious in having a second outer aisle on the north side, making three in all. There is a massive rood screen with painted panels, an interesting pulpit and brass eagle lectern very similar to the one in Wolborough Church.

From Bovey Tracey Church you walk through the village past buildings of many periods and architectural styles, keeping to the left at the former town hall, until you reach the bus stop where you should be able to catch a bus back to Newton Abbot.

Gleanings

New-bridge, where the Bovey river unites with the Teign, the views in every direction are delightful; and the river, having received the waters of many tributary streams and rills, which also flow from the mountain urn, assumes a formidable aspect, and sweeps in majestic grandeur to Teign-bridge, by which the Exeter road passes to Newton. On excavating the ground for taking down and rebuilding Teignbridge in 1815, the timbers of an ancient wooden bridge were discovered; and underneath, the piers of another bridge of white ashlar, apparently of Roman work. Rev. D.M. Stirling: *A History of Newton-Abbot and Newton-Bushel,* 1830

The **Heathfield** district to the South [of Bovey Tracey] was once a huge lake, which has been filled up by the detritus from the moor. This big alluvial flat, rich in china clay, provides potteries and brick-factories with work; but it must be owned that between this and Newton is the least picturesque spot in all Devon.
S.E. Winbolt: *Devon,* 1929

The valley of the Teign for some distance above Newton is a flat-bottomed basin rendered hideous by a continuous series of clay pits and made malodorous by the fumes of smouldering lignite turned up in the course of operations.
J.H. Wade: *Rambles in Devon,* 1930

The footpath way

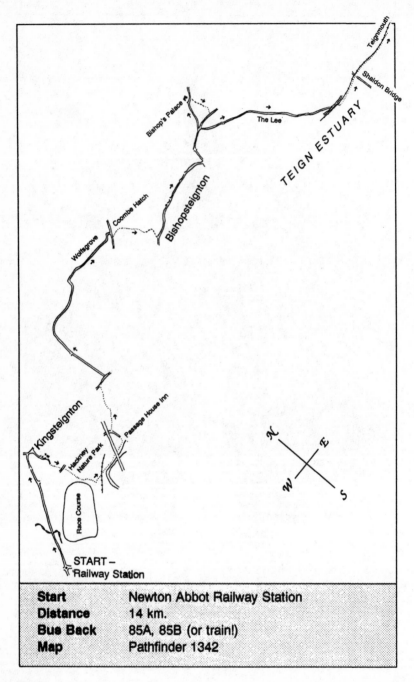

Teignmouth

Shaldon Bridge

TEIGN ESTUARY

Bishop's Palace

The Lee

Coombe Hatch

Bishopsteignton

Woltsgrove

Kingsteignton

Passage House Inn

Hackney Nature Park

Race Course

N
E
W
S

START –
Railway Station

Start	Newton Abbot Railway Station
Distance	14 km.
Bus Back	85A, 85B (or train!)
Map	Pathfinder 1342

11
NEWTON ABBOT - TEIGNMOUTH
via Kingsteignton, Hackney and Bishopsteignton

Going: Fairly easy; the first two miles and final mile are on the level. The highest altitude is 120 meters at Coombe Hatch, about half way, but this point is reached only after a few kilometeres steady ascent from Hackney. A bus may be taken from Newton Abbot to Kingsteignton if you wish to avoid the initial mile along a busy main road.

From Newton Abbot take the Kingsteignton Road and cross the Stover Canal, the railway line and the River Teign.

Some way past the entrance to Newton Abbot Race Course you will see a terrace of cottages built of the cream coloured bricks which are typical of Kingsteignton and, indeed, of Newton Abbot. These bricks were manufactured using the local ball clay in a factory which stood opposite this terrace of houses where the workers lived.

A little further along on the right hand side you will see the heavily buttressed walls of several former clay cellars where the dense, plastic ball clay was stored awaiting shipment by barge along the Hackney Canal and the Teign Estuary to the port of Teignmouth. These old clay cellars now comprise car repair workshops and the Hackney Canal has long since silted up.

Turn right at the junction opposite the service station and right again into Church Street and continue down here towards the Parish church. Your way is straight beside the lych gate to Kingsteignton Church, but it is worth first entering that gate.

St. Michael's Church has an imposing tower of grey limestone blocks of red sandstone, whilst the remainder of the church, with the exception of the south porch, is built of sandstone interspersed with limestone. Inside, a list of vicars gives the first as David in 1259. The church was entirely rebuilt in the fifteenth century. The lower parts of the rood screen can be seen either side of the chancel and are decorated with painted figures. There are some interesting memorial tablets: many of the seventeenth century set in the floors and other, more recent ones in the walls.

Outside in the churchyard you can see the leat or 'Fairwater', as it is known. This leat is said to have been dug by the Monks of Salisbury in the thirteenth century by channelling water which issued from springs in the limestone near Rydon towards the village in order to provide its inhabitants with a ready supply of drinking water as well as a source of energy. The leat disappears underground in front of the church tower. If you make for the churchyard wall to the right as you emerge from the porch you will see the rear of the Lower Mill and the leat issuing near a stationary water wheel.

This is an overshot water wheel. That is, the weight of water filling buckets attached at the top causes the wheel to rotate. The chute which carried the leat water has collapsed and the waters now fall uselessly to the lowest point of the wheel. Lower Mill was built in 1870 on the site of a much older mill, known as Norman Mill, thus forming a link with the alleged origin of the leat.

To continue walking, you should retrace your steps to the lych gate and turn left, past the mill, and carry straight on to a footpath junction. Turn left here beside the house gardens on your left, until you reach the road. Cross over and enter Hackney Marshes – Local Nature Park.

Bear right to follow the path along the right-hand boundary of the Park and beside Newton Abbot Race Course. Cross the footbridge and carry on beneath the main line railway bridge and over outcroppings of red tinted slate until, just before the new, concrete road bridge is reached, you find a number of ruined stone buildings.

Waterwheel at Kingsteignton

These are the remains of the village of Hackney, where lived the bargemen who plied the canal and estuary. These buildings are extremely dilapidated and overgrown but their walls display a great variety of building stone. There is grey limestone, red sandstone, greenstone and slate. This locality has a complex geology and that fact is certainly reflected in the walls of these old structures.

The Passage House Inn stands at the head of the Teign Estuary and the prospect from the car park is quite breathtaking. The wide expanse of water, or mud, depending upon the state of the tide, is flanked by the green and red field patchwork of hill and vale and, at the estuary's end, by the port of Teignmouth. There always seem to be cormorants on the hummocky islets just off shore, looking primeval as they dry their wings surrounded by the more numerous, sleek, efficient gulls.

Ruined cottage, Hackney

Turn up the lane between the pub and the hotel, over the railway line and then bear right up a cart track, initially concreted. You now begin to climb gently but steadily. Cross the Teignmouth Road and take the road opposite Wear Barton, one of the old houses of Kingsteignton. This road was widened when the nearby Kingsteignton bypass was built but, by the time you reach the first turning on the left, to Coombes End, the road has narrowed to a lane as it enters thickly wooded country.

You continue along this lane, past the entrances to a couple of disused quarries, a red brick lodge house and the thatched and pink washed farmhouse at Wolfsgrove until you reach the T-junction at Coombe's Hatch.

This longish stretch, although a public road, is quiet and peaceful and only very occasionally interrupted by motor traffic. Pauses are rewarded by a backward glance to the Dartmoor Hills.

At Coombe Hatch turn right and sharp left along a grassy track marked Public Footpath. Soon you enter a field by a five bar gate.

86

Here you will no doubt wish to sit and take in the spectacular prospect over Bishopsteignton and the Teign Estuary towards Ringmore and Shaldon and the hinterland beyond. There too is Teignmouth guarding all behind it from the sea.

Perhaps you will discover something of the variety of wild flowers that grow on this sunny bank. I once collected many samples but only managed to identify Ground Ivy with its square stem and purple flower, Dove's Foot Cranesbill, Bird's Eye Speedwell and Common Pearlwort.

Don't follow the well marked path to the right or left, which only leads to a gate marked 'Private', but head straight down the somewhat precipitous slope, into the thick of a plantation of beech trees – you will find a beaten path in their midst – and cross the stile at the bottom. Continue along the beaten path, over another stile, along the edge of a field by a brook, and through a gate to emerge at Brook Cottage. Here you take the track to the left which quite soon carries you to the main road into Bishopsteignton.

You walk along West Town and Fore Street and turn left up Radway Hill, then bear right into Radway Street. As you climb out of the village you will arrive at a junction at which the road branches into three. It is worth taking a short detour from our route to Teignmouth in order to investigate a feature on the O.S. map enticingly indicated in gothic script as 'Bishop's Palace (Remains of)'.

Sure enough, a little way up the left hand fork, in the midst of various farm buildings and agricultural implements, clearly discernible from the road and now featured on an information panel, can be seen an old wall with several lancet windows and a doorway. This and an adjoining wall are all that remain of a former Bishop's Palace.

Bishopsteignton belonged to the bishops of Exeter before the Norman Conquest and here they built one of their many 'Palaces', or country retreats. Bishop Grandisson, is a letter to Pope John 22nd., in 1332, describes the palace, which he is supposed to have built, as a 'beautiful structure'.

Bishop's Palace, Bishopsteignton

Turning back to the road, you continue by way of a cart track, the entrance to which lies almost opposite the ruined palace. The track bears right to become a narrow footpath. You climb over two stiles to emerge at Coombe Lane by the side of Coombe Cottages.

Turn right at Coombe Cottages, back to the junction where you branched off towards the Palace, and turn left up a narrow lane. This is known as The Lee, and is one of those Devon lanes so little used that grass grows along the middle. This elevated way follows a ridge and affords splendid views across the estuary, towards Shaldon, the Ness and the open sea.

Eventually it drops down to meet the main Teignmouth-Newton Abbot road. BE VERY CAREFUL how you cross here – the road to the right is rather blind. Head straight across the bridge directly opposite, over the railway and bear left beside the estuary. This right of way takes you under the Shaldon road bridge and up to the Western Quay and bustling dockside scene.

Gleanings

Kingsteignton has a pleasing appearance from the many parts of the circumjacent country and is for the most part inhabited by persons under the clay company.
Rev. D. M. Stirling
A History of Newton-Abbot and Newton-Bushel, 1830

At *Hackney* is held annually a regatta, at which, exciting events are keenly contested to the amusement and edification of hundreds of spectators. At such times mine host at the inn, with upturned sleeves and perspiring face, dispenses beer and cockles to the sturdy bargmen and clay cutters.
Talks on walks in and around Newton Abbot, c. 1905

Bishopsteignton is a village of considerable magnitude, delightfully situated on the north bank of the River Teign ... In the village and its vicinity, reside many families of great respectability. The prospect from Bishopsteignton is extensive, and the scenery discriminated inexpressibly beautiful and romantic.
Rev D. M. Stirling
A History of Newton-Abbot and Newton-Bushel, 1830

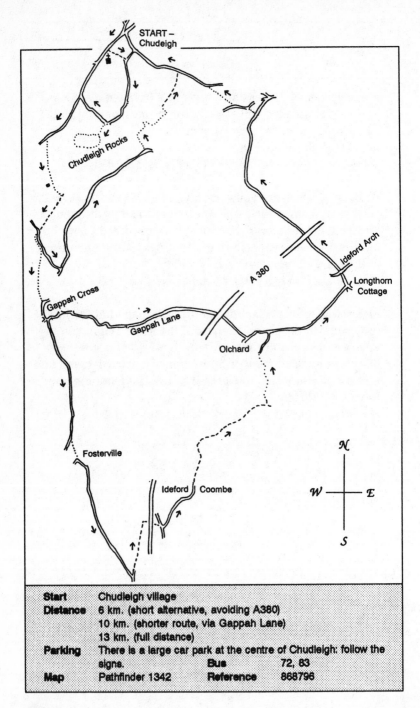

START –
Chudleigh

Chudleigh Rocks

Ideford Arch

Longthorn
Cottage

A 380

Gappah Cross

Gappah Lane

Olchard

Fosterville

Ideford Coombe

N
W   E
S

Start	Chudleigh village
Distance	6 km. (short alternative, avoiding A380)
	10 km. (shorter route, via Gappah Lane)
	13 km. (full distance)
Parking	There is a large car park at the centre of Chudleigh: follow the signs. **Bus** 72, 83
Map	Pathfinder 1342 **Reference** 868796

12
CHUDLEIGH CIRCULAR

via Chudleigh Rocks, Gappah Cross, Ideford Combe and Arch
Shorter route, avoiding A380, via boundary of Ugbrooke Park

Going: This is a fairly easy ramble with few steep inclines. The going can be heavy in wet weather, particularly in Well Covert. A shorter alternative route is possible, via Gappah Lane; this avoids a lengthy southern loop but if you choose this route you will miss the descent to Ideford Combe, as well as the footpath from here to Olchard Lane. The one hazard on this ramble, by the shorter or longer route, is the A380, now a fast dual carriageway, which has to be crossed. If you really wish to avoid this (and I strongly suggest you do if you have children with you), a second alternative, much shorter route is described first.

As you emerge from the car park at the war memorial, turn right along the main street towards the church on the left. Just before the entrance gate to the churchyard you take the footpath on the left. When you reach the lane turn right, down past the Old Mill House on the Kate Brook and then begin to climb – notice the quarry face across the valley to your left.

At Glen Cottage the lane takes a right bend. Just past this point look out for an iron kissing gate on the left; this leads to a narrow path towards Chudleigh Rocks, an impressive cliff of Devonian Limestone. Some scrambling will be necessary here, but the drama of these cliffs and caves is well worth the effort.

Chudleigh Rocks is the product of years of quarrying the fine grey stone – it was used both as building stone and for firing in kilns. The caves have been excavated and were found to have been inhabited both by early man and by animals long since extinct. They are now, apparently, the home of rare bats.

Unfortunately, there is no exit from the Rocks at their western extremity. It is possible to walk through the grounds of Chudleigh Rock Activity Centre but this is private property so cannot be recommended. Retrace your steps to the kissing gate and then turn left at the lane, then left at the main road. Shortly past the Activity Centre look out for a Public Footpath sign and kissing gate on the left. Enter the field here, leave the road behind you, and descend towards the house by the beaten path. Now the right of way rises and bears right along a rough track beside a wood. Be sure to look back for a full frontal view of Chudleigh Rocks.

Chudleigh Rocks

Shorter route, avoiding the A380, via boundary of Ugbrooke Lane: When you reach the lane bear left, then turn left at the T-junction, where you follow the lane along the boundary wall of Ugbrooke Park on your right and woods on your left. At the end of the wood look out for a Public Footpath sign on the left. Follow the right of way as it descends the hill and then veers to the right. Go through a kissing gate, follow the hedge to another, and another. Turn left to reach a track, then turn right to reach the lane.

Turn left and carry straight on past the Wheel Craft Centre and along Clifford Street to reach your starting point.

Resuming the longer routes via the A380:

When you reach the lane, cross over and climb the step stile opposite to enter a field. Bear left immediately to follow the hedgerow to another stile close by, and follow the path beside the lane to reach a third stile. Now bear a little to the right to reach a gap in the hedgerow on the far side. Tack across this sloping field towards the hedgerow which you follow on your right to reach the lane. Follow the lane straight ahead to Gappah Cross.

Alternative shorter route via Gappah Lane:

Head down the lane which descends past the farm buildings to the left. Follow the lane for about a mile until you reach the A380. Cross the road (take great care!) and continue for a short distance on the far side until you reach Olchard Lane at a T-junction where you turn left.

Resuming the longer route:

Take the lane signposted to Fosterville and Kingsteignton. After some way look out for a Public Footpath sign on the left – the right of way cuts across a flint-strewn field and cuts off an awkward corner. Head just to the left of the thatched cottage where you reach the lane once more. Cross the Ugbrooke Stream, (a splendid display of marsh marigold and lady's smock grows in the meadow here) and bear right along the lane below the wooded hillside. Quite soon it is possible to get off the tarmac and walk along the gorsey bank on the left or beside the concrete channel on the far side.

Eventually the lane reaches the new houses of Kingsteignton – here you turn sharp left up a redundant lane as far as a notice declaring 'Danger – Quarry Workings'. Turn right towards the fence. Climb over and, with the greatest caution, cross the A380. The track continues directly opposite and soon reaches the former main road. Cross over and descend by the lane signposted to Ideford Combe. Soon you will enjoy the view across the orchards of Combe Holdridge Farm. Just past the farm entrance you bear left, below the cottages and woods, to follow a muddy track up a valley. Eventually you will meet a stout, recently constructed wooden bridge which leads across the stream. Cross here and follow the path uphill until you reach the buildings by a wooden gate. Bear left, pass through an iron gate, then keep bearing right until you reach a lane. Turn right here.

Views through the high hedgebanks here will reveal large, straight-edged and gently sloping fields which seem uncharacteristic of South Devon. On the horizons ahead and to your right are the twin ridges of Great Haldon and Little Haldon, covered with forest and heath respectively.

Follow the lane to the junction at Longthorn Cottage – the thatched, rubble-stone walled, rustic looking property directly opposite. From this point you begin your return to Chudleigh. Turn left, under Ideford Arch, a Georgian flyover which was built in 1810 to carry the new turnpike road from Exeter. Continue under the A380, past the impressive entrance to the grounds of Ugbrooke House.

Ugbrooke House has been the home of the Lords Clifford since the sixteenth century, although the present house dates from the eighteenth century. The house and grounds are open to the public in the summer months.

Continue by the lane as it bears right below the hanging wood on your left and valley to your right. Keep your eyes skinned for a narrow gap in the greenery on your left, directly above the house on your right. Follow the path up through the wood to reach the lane. Bear left, then leave the lane by taking the indicated Public Footpath on the right. Descend

Gatepost at Ugbrooke

the slope from here towards Chudleigh, the large village attractively spread out among trees and hedgerows half a mile or so ahead. When you join the lane carry straight on, past the Wheel Craft Centre – Clifford Street with its old cottages will lead you to the road junction at Chudleigh's centre.

Gleanings

Chudleigh Rock, rising on the skirts of Ugbrooke, and presenting naked surfaces of stone, which are seen here and there in the gaps of a wild and irregular wood, and at the summit form platforms, commanding the most delightful views. Within this marble barrier is a glen, where trees grow tangled; and a brawling stream, concealed from sunshine by the foliage, runs murmuring by its moss-grown stones, and, at one point, leaps in a cascade, which from below looks like the keep of a castle, is bound, as it were, with creepers, and has open spots (commanding wide views) on the summit, on which wild fennel grows luxuriantly; midway on the cliff is the mouth of a cavern which the country people describe as haunted by the Pixies.

John Murray: *A Handbook for Travellers in Devonshire,* 1887

Early next morning the wind blowing mild, but misty, from the south-west, and threatening rain, we proceeded [from **Chudleigh**] to Ashburton; about half a mile on this road hang the rude heads of a large black marble rock, which commands a wild view of the hills, woods and vales beneath; this curious stratum, found in large bodies in this part of the country, we saw here converted by fire into very useful lime for dressing and improving the land, a great part of which is arable and pasture, as well as abounds in cyder fruits, this year so uncommonly plentiful. In these marble quarries they get large blocks, and send them to Plymouth, London, etc. which for hardness and variety of veins are little inferior to foreign productions.

Rev. S. Shaw: *A Tour to the West of England in 1788,* 1789

Other books by Roger Jones:

A BOOK OF NEWTON ABBOT
This is the third edition of the book which first appeared in 1979, and deals with various aspects of the town's history.
'This book must be assured of a permanent place in any bookshelf or library as a continual source of pleasure and of reference for future use' – *Devon Life*
147 pages; map; photographs and drawings   Price £3.95

BETWIXT MOOR AND SEA
Rambles in South Devon
Only one of the routes described in this book duplicates one of those in *Rambles around Newton Abbot*, but there are fourteen others to choose from which begin at Harbertonford, Marldon, Totnes, Broadhempston, Cornworthy, Dittisham, Diptford, Ermington, Modbury, Kingston, Loddiswell, Malborough, West Charlton and Slapton.
'Walkers following the routes described will be taken into a quiet and still largely unspoilt corner of the country ... a lengthy introduction sets the scene, dealing with geology, people in the landscape and place names ... none of the routes are over-strenuous and most are well waymarked.'
– *The Great Outdoors*
93 pages; maps and sketches   Price £2.95

GREEN ROAD TO LAND'S END
Diary of a Journey on Foot from London to Land's End
141 pages; sketch maps and pen and ink drawings; Price £2.95

In addition to the above titles, Ex Libris Press publishes a range of books on West Country topics as well as some general titles, and we are continually adding new books to our list.
Ex Libris books may be obtained through your local bookshop or direct from the publisher, post-free, on receipt of net price, at
1 The Shambles, Bradford on Avon, Wiltshire, BA15 1JS